LEADING WITH SELF-AWARENESS

Starting from the Inside Out

CURATED BY CHANGING WORK

SCOTT SHUTE   NICHOLAS WHITAKER
KWAME OSAGYEFO   JENNIFER LESLIE   AIMEE SERENE
RACHAEL O'MEARA   LORI SCHWANBECK   JEFF JACOBS
ANNA OAKES   NICOLE ELIAS SEAWELL
CHRISTINE WENGER   NELL DERICK DEBEVOISE
WILDER HORNG BRAWER   LISA FOULGER
MISSY BRIGHT   QUENTIN FINNEY   TRICIA LIVERMORE
TERI SWOPE   ALEC KASSIN   WENDY MCHENRY
MATT MCLAUGHLIN   DÉSIRÉE PASCUAL
JILL SANTERCIER   EMMA LAURENCE   TIM VAN NESS
COURTNEY FEIDER   KATHERINE TWELLS   EARL TALBOT

LEADING WITH SELF-AWARENESS: STARTING FROM THE INSIDE OUT

© 2024 Changing Work

All Rights Reserved. Apart from any fair dealing for the purposes of research or private study, or criticism or review, as permitted under the Copyright, Designs and Patents Act 1988, this publication may only be reproduced, stored or transmitted, in any form or by any means, with the prior permission in writing of the copyright owner, or in the case of the reprographic reproduction in accordance with the terms of licenses issued by the Copyright Licensing Agency. Enquiries concerning reproduction outside those terms should be sent to the publisher.

Editor: Lisa Thomas-Tench

Copy Editor: Joshua Humphreys

Layout: Natalie Lapre

Print ISBN: 979-8-9911984-0-0

Ebook ISBN: 979-8-9911984-1-7

Contents

Foreword   vii
Garry Ridge

A Letter from Scott and Nick   xi

Believing and Belonging

1. SHAFT   3
   Kwame Osagyefo (Gaylon Logan, Jr.)

2. BE BOLD, LIEUTENANT!   13
   Jennifer Leslie

3. INTEGRATING THE MOMENTS OF MYSTICAL SELF-SURRENDER   21
   Aimee Serene

4. BEYOND MYSELF   29
   Rachael O'Meara

5. BIGGER: ACCESSING THE WISDOM OF THE EXPANDED SELF   37
   Lori Schwanbeck

Embracing Your Change

6. WHAT INMATES CAN TEACH US ABOUT VULNERABILITY   47
   Jeff Jacobs

7. LEVERAGING SELF-AWARENESS FOR CAREER IMPACT   55
   Anna Oakes

8. YOUR REALITY IS WHAT THE OTHER PERSON THINKS YOU SAID   63
   Nicole Elias Seawell

9. FINDING MY EARLY WARNING SIGNAL   71
   Christine Wenger

10. THE STINK OF MISALIGNMENT   79
    Nell Derick Debevoise

Living Authentically

11. UNBOUND Wilder Horng Brawer	91
12. OPENING DOORS TO DISCOVER ME Lisa Foulger	99
13. LIVING YOUR TRUTH Missy Bright	107
14. PERFECTLY GOOD ENOUGH Quentin Finney	115
15. FROM INNER CRITIC TO INNER PEACE Tricia Livermore	123

Coming Back from the Edge

16. THE UNREVEALED MASTERPIECE WITHIN Teri Swope	133
17. FROM PAIN MANAGEMENT TO PAIN FREE Alec Kassin	141
18. FROM PINK SLIP TO INNER CALM Wendy McHenry	149
19. FROM PANIC ATTACKS TO SELF-DISCOVERY Matt McLaughlin	157
20. FEEL THE BURN Désirée Pascual & Jill Santercier	165

Opening to Wonder

21. PASTA POETICA Emma Laurence	175
22. CHOOSE YOUR STORY Tim Van Ness	183
23. THE ADVENTURE OF SLOWING DOWN Courtney Feider	191
24. BRIDGING WORLDS Katherine Twells	199
25. OPERATING FROM YOUR ZONE OF GENIUS Earl Talbot	207
Afterword	215
About Changing Work	221

Foreword

Garry Ridge

In my years as CEO of WD-40 Company, I had the privilege of witnessing firsthand the transformative power of leadership that is both compassionate and self-aware. This experience led me to establish The Learning Moment, helping to build other learning and empowering organizational cultures; and to support, collaborate with, and lift up others doing like-minded work.

Among these, the Changing Work Collective (CWC) is a powerful new initiative that I particularly appreciate because of its inclusive operating model, which pulls in wisdom from a diverse group of leadership practitioners, experts, and coaches. Changing Work is a movement deeply committed to revolutionizing the dynamics of the workplace from within. Their vision is simple yet profound: to change work from the inside out.

In my own next book, *Any Dumbass Can Do It*, I share my learning moments as CEO of a multibillion-dollar, global company. Because of my deep belief that every individual in a company is a leader, I am thrilled to support CWC's first book, *Leading with Self-Awareness*. The book's co-authored model provides the array of perspectives required to speak to the diverse range of leaders who shape the twenty-first-century workforce.

The world is at a crossroads, facing unprecedented changes in our professional and personal lives. This cultural and work environment demands a shift towards greater self-awareness and compassion. Command-and-control, industrial-era approaches to leadership do not work. We need new approaches that recognize the holistic nature of human beings and the interconnectedness of our lives and work.

The good news is that these new approaches are not rocket science—*Any Dumbass Can Do It!*—and they start with self-awareness, described in a wonderfully firsthand way by the CWC authors in this volume. I frequently quote Aristotle, who is credited with saying, "Pleasure in the job puts perfection in the work." True pleasure comes from knowing the things that bring us joy, and so the journey to know ourselves is a critical foundation for effective leadership.

This book is for everyone committed to creating a workplace where you go to work each day, make a contribution to something bigger than yourself, learn something new, feel safe, are protected, are provided freedom by a set of values, and go home happy!

Whether you are a seasoned leader, emerging professional, coach, consultant, or a curious human seeking greater fulfillment, this book offers valuable insights and practical wisdom. So many of us are struggling today, seeking new ways to navigate the complexities of modern work and life. This book can help by sharing widely varied stories of others' journeys of self-awareness, offering guidance, inspiration, and a sense of shared humanity.

Leading with Self-Awareness is a collaborative effort, featuring 25 chapters authored by individuals who have each embarked on their unique journey of self-awareness. The book is divided into five parts: Believing and Belonging, Embracing Your Change, Living Authentically, Coming Back from the Edge, and Opening to Wonder. This structure allows readers to resonate with different authors and stories, seeing themselves reflected in the diverse experiences shared.

As you delve into this book, I encourage you to approach it with an open heart and mind. The stories and insights contained within these pages are not just about leadership at work, but about leading ourselves throughout our lives with self-awareness and compassion. In doing so, we can create workplaces that enable people to feel purposeful, challenged, safe, fulfilled, and free. Together, we can change work from the inside out, building successful companies where everyone can thrive.

Thank you for joining us on this journey.

Garry Ridge
Chairman Emeritus, WD-40 Company
& The Culture Coach

A Letter from Scott and Nick

Yesterday I was clever, and I tried to change the world. Today I am wise and I'm changing myself.

—Rumi

What if our cultures at work were so good they actually helped people heal?

What if every leader and every board achieved their profit goals by ensuring all their stakeholders, not just shareholders, were successful?

We founded Changing Work because we're dreamers. Maybe you have the same dream. We want work to be a better experience for more people. We want the work we do to matter.

We want to change work from the inside out.

We've seen amazing workplaces, filled with compassion, trust, and psychological safety. They are beautiful, but rare. We've also seen it go poorly. Unbelievably poorly! So have you.

These work cultures, these companies, are just collections of individuals. They are reflections of us, of our strengths and weaknesses, our greed, and our courage. Workplaces are a mirror of our consciousness.

Yes, we want the workplace to change. We want the workplace to be somewhere we all feel safe, where we can do our best and most creative and meaningful work. A place where we build community and purpose. A place where everyone is treated with respect, dignity, and compassion. A place where the best of our nature is encouraged and embraced. We want the workplace to be somewhere we do hard things in support of the whole. And yes, of course, we'll still do this while being profitable. But instead of profit being the only measure that matters we'll also measure our impact on the broader community we live in.

When we ask ourselves, "Does our work matter?" we want to say YES!

Workplace culture also matters. Workplaces have become incredibly influential on our consciousness. If we go to work at a big company, we have to fit into the culture or we won't be successful. These companies and their cultural norms influence how we think and how we act towards our customers and each other. They are shaping our consciousness in ways that governments and religions have been doing for thousands of years.

Changing work for the 3.5 billion people in the global workforce can seem daunting. But actually it's pretty easy. It just requires each one of us to make some small changes. It starts from the inside out.

It starts with our own self-awareness.

It starts with making this personal.

What about you? Why did you pick this book up in the first place?

Perhaps this notion is already stirring inside you. "There's got to be more," you may be saying to yourself. "There has to be more to this life than just toiling for profit."

What would it look like for you if your work had more purpose? If you felt like you were making the world a better place each day with your efforts? If you built something you would be proud to pass on to the next generation?

We have something to share with you.

A Letter from Scott and Nick

The stories that follow are written by twenty-five unique and amazing humans. The idea for this book is simple: twenty-five experts from our Changing Work community each writing a chapter on self-awareness. Each one of them is the global expert in *being them*, just like you are the leading expert in *being you*. Each one tells a story that's deeply important to them and their journey of self-awareness. These lessons are hard-earned and poignant.

Lean in closely and you'll see yourself in their stories.

As a community, we don't have all the answers. No one does. In fact, if they claim to, it's a red flag.

Essentially, our understanding of conscious business, of life, of work, even of spirituality, is more of a question. It's a journey, more than a destination. Writing a book together is a way of deepening our own personal and collective understanding of the topic. This book can be used to further the conversation both inside our Changing Work community and in the wider workplace.

Each of these writers has learned through experience a great deal about their own self-awareness. By going through the writing process, they've each deepened their own understanding of their journey. Sharing that understanding with the rest of us, we gain a chance to reflect on our own life. Are we conscious? What does that even mean?

We're in a territory in which there's no right or wrong, no definitive text to consult. Consciousness is a subjective experience. There's no degree, no certification to be had. No outside force can provide us with a score or a level. It's up to us, each one of us, to know ourselves and to choose every day to evolve.

Each one of us has the opportunity to ask inside, "Who am I? Do I want more than this? How do I really want to live? How do I want to show up in the world? What impact do I want to have on others? What would a better version of me look like?"

Our dream is that this book moves the discussion of conscious business and conscious leadership forward. That it leads you to ponder your own path, your own actions. That the actions you take inspire others to evolve as well. Over time, each of these small changes creates a movement. In that movement, we all benefit.

A Letter from Scott and Nick

One thing is super clear to us. If we want to change work, if we want to change the world, it starts with each one of us—from within.

Scott Shute
Nicholas Whitaker
Founders, Changing Work

Believing and Belonging

ONE

Shaft

Kwame Osagyefo (Gaylon Logan, Jr.)

"Rusty! Rusty!"

Slowly awakening from my sleep and recognizing my grandmother's voice, the appetizing aroma of bacon filled my nostrils. The unmistakable seasoning of her breakfast potatoes, onions, scrambled eggs, and toasted bread permeated the air. This was a daily morning spread that, to this day, could not be matched by anyone else, at home or at a restaurant.

I could see a faint glimmer of dawn peeking through the small window in my room, a regular occurrence since my grandmother would wake up early to prepare breakfast for my grandfather. She enlisted me as her assistant. My grandfather arrived home religiously every morning at 7 a.m., as he operated two 24-hour social clubs in West Phoenix. It wasn't until much later in life that I discovered the fronts of the social clubs were made up of pool tables, pinball machines, and a dining area. Yet in the back, another world existed that catered to more mature adult needs: gambling, drug dealing, prostitution.

"Rusty! Boy, I'm not going to call you again."

Now fully awake, I could hear agitation in her voice and knew from experience that my grandmother meant business.

"Ok G'Ma! I'm getting up!"

I slowly arose and went through the process of getting dressed and washing up. At six years old this routine had become woven into the fabric of my subconscious. Entering the kitchen, I caught site of my grandmother darting throughout the kitchen with the skill and grace of a master chef—a short, thickly built fair-skinned woman with long beautiful black hair. Within the black community, many would consider her a redbone. Her name was Zipporah, I simply called her G'Ma, and most other people called her Mrs. Logan.

That morning, she was partly humming and singing a Mahalia Jackson gospel song,

"I wanna thank him for how he brought me (Humm Humm), And I wanna thank God for how he taught me (oh yes), Oh thank my God how he kept me (Humm Humm)."

I loved her silky sweet voice and learned to gauge her moods by the nuance of her singing.

"MAMA," MY FATHER had said to my grandmother years earlier. "I need to have a conversation with you and Dad. I ain't been able to catch him at the club, but I need to go to San Francisco with Betty and the kids this weekend since we just found an apartment and can move in next week."

"Wait, what about your court case that's coming up in a few weeks?"

"Yeah, I'm gonna deal with it, but Mama I know they gon' give me some time. I can't go back to jail right now! I wanna get on my feet and focus on taking care of my family."

At two years old, I was oblivious to my parents moving us around due to my father's drug addiction and the illegal actions that supported his habit.

"I need to know if you could look after Gaylon for a bit," my father said, referring to me by my birth name. "We can only afford a one-bedroom right now and it'll be easier for us without him."

"I'll talk to Big John and see how he feels about this, but

regardless of what he says I need you to finally make up your mind and put an end to this recklessness. You can't keep running these streets, you got a family now."

"Mama, I'm tired of running with these fools and getting in trouble."

She replied with heaviness and uncertainty: "I understand son, but remember, they have streets in California too."

My father's request for my grandparents to care for me for a short period of time turned into four years. I would sometimes wonder if they were having fun without me, what did I do wrong not to have been taken, and at the root of my questions; why they didn't want me? Usually, the thoughts would come and go, but there were moments where not knowing became too much, and in these moments I would cry in my grandmother's arms, asking why to my insistent questions.

"Rusty!" she would say, "There's a lot you just won't understand right now. Just know that your mom and dad do love you very much, and you'll be with them soon."

Whenever my grandmother spoke those words I would find peace, and return to my routine of house chores, attending school, watching cartoons, and building model cars. While I can't recall one defining moment, as a child I came to the realization that *somebody genuinely loved me*. It took years to comprehend just how influential my grandmother's persistent encouragement, unyielding dedication to structure, and exceptional cooking were in shaping the person I am today.

ONE MORNING, just three weeks before my eighth birthday, while eating breakfast I sensed that something was troubling my grandmother. Her usual singing was absent, and she seemed preoccupied as she moved around the house. A few times I noticed her staring at me, which made me uneasy.

"Rusty, your mom and dad will be here this weekend," she finally said.

Though I felt excited and happy at first, I could tell that there was more to it than what she was saying.

"They're taking you back to California to live with them," she finally revealed.

I was numb, a flood of contradictory emotions took over my senses. The realization of being reunited with my family filled me with pure joy and anticipation, yet the fear of the unknown hovered over me like a dark cloud.

The ten-hour journey from Phoenix to San Francisco was a blend of new experiences and confusion for me. I found myself cramped in a steel box with four strangers whom, despite having met occasionally in the past, I had never really spent time with. My father remained mostly silent, leaving any significant communication to my mother. She made attempts to ask about my school, my friends, and the travel bag my grandmother had given me, which included toys, books, and a Superman watch.

"Junior, do you like working on puzzles?" my mother asked.

I could sense the unease in her voice, and I wished she would stop trying. At that time, I lacked the insight to comprehend a mother trying to connect with a child she didn't know.

"Junior, are you hungry?"

My name was Gaylon Jr., but everyone had been calling me Rusty. My grandmother gave me the nickname because, she said, when I was born I looked like a rusty nail. I responded, realizing that I needed to adjust to this new identity. On that journey north, I was squished in the back seat between my brother Gary and my sister Micky, which felt like both a good and bad thing. My brother seemed displeased about my presence and elbowed me repeatedly during the long ride. In contrast, my sister hugged me often and expressed how happy she was to see me. This proved to be one of the longest rides of my life.

A few days after arriving at my new home, two small speakers in the living room blared the chart-topping Stevie Wonder song, "Superstition,"

"*When you believe in things that you don't understand, then you suffer, superstition ain't the way."* Years later the meaning of that song would weigh heavily on my personal journey.

It was a Saturday morning, and I had just finished getting dressed, completing my cleaning tasks, and gobbling down a bowl of cereal. House-cleaning was a family routine that always involved music, mainly R&B and jazz.

"Mama, can I go outside?"

I was hoping to join the usual crew for a game of football on the street. Afterwards a few of us typically set out to explore parts of the neighborhood we had not yet seen. It had been over two months since leaving behind the comfortable routine of Phoenix and the abundance of food and love. But on this day of football, my father called me outside and pointed to a boy standing in the courtyard.

"Go whip his ass!" my father yelled.

I couldn't think, I couldn't feel, and he might as well have been speaking Chinese. My father's intention was for me to fight someone on purpose, yet without purpose—for me at least. I didn't understand! Fight, flight, or freeze! I recall it seeming like the whole neighborhood was watching. I was undoubtably frozen and would have given anything to sprout wings and fly as far away as I could get. I did not want to fight but in that moment the luxury of choice was absent.

Needless to say, I got my ass kicked that day.

There would be many more fighting matches, which I now realize served a purpose at the time. But for that eight-year-old kid it just didn't feel normal.

ONE SATURDAY I was exploring the neighborhood with my crew, with no idea that the day would introduce me to a vital supporter in my quest for cultural assimilation. I noticed a dog digging through an overturned garbage can, a stray dog with a scruffy, brownish-gray fur coat with patches of white mixed in, medium-sized, with a lean and muscular build. His tail was long and thin, with a crook at the end, and his ears were perked up as if always alert to his surroundings. As I got closer to him I could see his eyes were a dark brown and his muzzle was triangular and pointed. His paws were rough and callused, indicating that he may have been wandering the streets for some time.

Despite his unkempt appearance, he had a gentle and friendly demeanor, often wagging his tail and seeking attention from anyone who might offer it. As our crew got closer to him he immediately stood alert ready to stay or flee.

"That's Shaft," one of the boys said to no one in particular, affirming merely that he knew the dog.

Suddenly angry voices erupted from a distance, drawing our group's attention in another direction. As was customary in the neighborhood, seeing a fight was perceived as entertaining. As the group headed towards the disturbance I continued to approach the dog who had been observing us.

"Hey boy!" I called out, and he warily watched me as I neared him. I could see his various battle scars up close, which deepened my understanding of the abuse he had endured. At about five feet away from him I stopped and lowered myself to one knee. Slowly Shaft advanced, sensing that I posed no threat. I petted his head gently. "Good boy, good boy."

He eagerly responded, craving human touch. The rank, putrid smell of his breath evidenced his lack of care and poor dental health. "Damn, your breath stank!"

On that day Shaft followed me home and I managed to sneak two hot dogs from our refrigerator to feed him. In the months that followed he became a regular presence in my daily routine. I realized quickly that with limited food at home, I had to sneak whatever food I might manage to give him. Often, I had to share portions of my meals with him and however small the portion, Shaft would always find a way to supplement his diet by scavenging from neighbors' trash cans.

My acculturation process was undoubtedly challenging. Phoenix, with its lavish, fulfilling meals and my grandmother's uplifting presence and soulful singing, now felt like a million miles away. I could feel myself growing harder emotionally and mentally as I adapted to the poverty, the pain, and the violence that had become the norm for me. I could feel myself transforming into someone different, but it was a change that was beyond my control.

As days passed, Shaft became a permanent resident, sleeping in a crawl space beneath our unit. Sometimes, I would look outside my window at night to see him staring up at me, his tail wagging vigorously as if he was trying to communicate something important.

Shaft seemed to sense my inner turmoil and became to me a reminder that despite my circumstances I was loved for who I was, and not for what I did. I truly could hear my grandmother hum and sing through Shaft. Yes, Shaft was my reminder.

IT HAD BEEN MORE than a week since I last spotted Shaft and my worry began to grow.

I reminded myself of how adept he was at navigating the dangerous streets of Hunter's Point, which temporarily calmed my anxious thoughts. It was an uncharacteristically hot day, and after we finished a game of football, I was thoroughly drenched in sweat. I had just told the guys that I was going home to get some cold Kool-Aid and would catch up with them later when a car sped by at a ridiculous speed. Within seconds we heard the sound of screeching tires. I anticipated a dreadful metal-to-metal impact but instead I heard a dull thud and the whimper of a dog. The acrid smoke from the burning rubber drifted towards us, accompanied by a chorus of anguished yells from the approaching crowd.

I sprinted towards the scene as fast as I could, which in reality was only about a block away. As I reached the spot I saw the car speed off into the distance, leaving behind a small group of people huddling over a wriggling and bleeding Shaft, gasping for air and trying to hold on to his life.

My heart sank as I realized he was beyond help.

A strange, inexplicable compulsion made me flee from the scene as fast as I could. I heard one of the guys calling out, asking where I was going, and on an impulse I yelled back, "My mama's calling me!"

I ran, tears streaming down my face, grief and sorrow tightening my heart with each step.

IT HAD BEEN twenty years since Shaft entered my life, and I found myself thinking about him once more.

One day my mentor, Le Roy Gillead, a Tuskegee Airman from Brooklyn, asked me a thought-provoking question: "What is your purpose in life?"

I had never truly contemplated the purpose of my existence up until that point. I was raised with the belief that I needed to "do" something in order to "have" something and only then would I be considered valuable. This indoctrinated narrative consumed me and I had never thought beyond it.

It was only when Le Roy posed this question that I realized the true meaning of my existence and the fact that everything in life has a purpose.

Shaft came into my life at a crucial time—a time when my sense of identity was still taking shape and my beliefs were influencing my perception of myself, my family, and the world. I came to understand that our principles are guided by our values and that they in turn guide us toward our purpose in life. But what happens when we're unsure of our purpose, or misguided in our values?

Shaft provided me with a vital reminder of who I truly was and what really mattered. He opened up a world of humanity to me—a world of freedom from judgment, ridicule, and shame. His presence served as a beacon of hope amidst the poverty, violence, and pain that surrounded us.

Reflecting on this experience poses the questions: In what ways do we compromise our humanity? Are our core values aligned with our principles? It's important to ask ourselves these questions, to ensure that we remain true to who we are and what we believe.

Just as Shaft provided me with much-needed clarity, we must also strive to stay on the path that aligns our values with the principles that guide us on our journey towards purpose and fulfillment.

Shaft

Kwame Osagyefo (Gaylon Logan, Jr.)

Kwame Osagyefo is the founder and CEO of Village-Connect, an award-winning San Francisco Bay Area organization. Village-Connect is a comprehensive integrated system of care that employs transformative coaching in helping individuals, families, and communities to heal, grow, and to achieve social, economic, emotional, and political sustainability. For more than twenty-five years Kwame has served the community as a thought-leader, an organizational development consultant, a workshop and seminar facilitator, Master CBTC coach, and as a motivational speaker who delivers profound perspectives on fatherhood and on motivating youth and families towards success.

TWO

Be Bold, Lieutenant!

Jennifer Leslie

The Monterey Bay fog has not yet burned off. Nothing ever dries here in this season, I'm certain my bath towel will still be damp tomorrow when I get out of the shower. The lavender is in full bloom and I'm happy to be home.

I'm staying at my parents' house and it's a Sunday morning, so of course we're off to church. My dad is a retired Episcopalian priest and happily does supply work around the Diocese of El Camino Real, which is kind of like substitute teaching. We are a mixed-up reverent bunch. My mom is Catholic, my husband is Jewish, and I've had a daily meditation practice for five years. I find peace in religious spaces. In tradition. In the kindness of spiritual people. And on this particular Sunday morning I'm looking forward to hearing my dad preach.

Back at my other home on the east coast, work has been feeling like rush hour all day long. The operational bits, mechanical and rote, are making me keenly aware that I've lost my spark, forgotten my "so what." Climbing into the back seat, heading to church, was like ducking into a time machine. Even in my late forties, I was right there, back in childhood.

When we're kids we begin building a personal library:

collections of stories, anecdotes, and tales—sometimes tall, sometimes told by others from a time before we were born. If I close my eyes I can picture the stories from my childhood as hardcover books, stacked one on top of the other like bricks. They create a fortress from where I defend my borders. They are a starting point for how I understand myself in contrast to the outside world.

Attachment parenting was all the rage when my kids were babies. Breastfeeding made a comeback. I'm embarrassed by the volume of parenting and self-help books I read. I was desperate for a user guide. An FAQ. A skip-to-recipe would have been nice so I could just get on with it! What I know now is there are no shortcuts, no hard-and-fast rules, and no matter what, we do get stuck and sticky with where we're from. We mimic what we see. We try on grown-up words and we learn to harvest or fly airplanes or file legal briefs or give sermons. We watch the behavior and posturing and language of those closest to us and we attach to what we see.

Then sometimes we don't. Or won't.

Sometimes we feel lost, and wander around the hallways and winding passages of our bodies and minds in search of who we want to be, separate from all that was patterned for us. Sometimes the pilot episode doesn't woo us and we mount our horse and ride into the countryside in search of our people. In search of our magic.

BALANCING AGAINST THE WAVES, I've spent the past few years excavating and elevating my voice.

In the early days I would wonder "Where did it get stuck in the first place?" I imagined myself as a pirate on the bow of a ship extending my handheld telescope out from my one open eye, sizing up a distant land. I could see my own rebellion as a teenager coupled with a fear of being seen as anything other than perfect. This sometimes played itself out in me climbing out of my bedroom window late at night but being extraordinarily cautious about not getting into any serious trouble. There was no throwing caution to the wind—I've spent most of my life being cautious—which is part of what held me back as a leader. My innate need for balance,

Be Bold, Lieutenant!

balancing my desire to push boundaries along with keeping my world safe, made for one very static see-saw.

On the flip side, navigating my preacher's kid persona also came with a lot of perks. I enjoyed instant acceptance and adoration within our church community. We were the popular kids without having to try. There was also regular validation of my existence, by way of hearing my name, or something clever, or not so clever, that I'd done in the week leading up to Sunday's sermon. I loved being the center of the story and was jealous whenever one of my brothers was the focus that day. Watching and listening to my dad, week after week, I learned to crave stories.

My dad was in the ROTC in college and after being stationed in Germany, where I was born, he went to seminary on the GI bill. He continued to serve in the army as a chaplain while also being a parish priest. His sermon, that fog-laden California morning, was in response to a Bible reading that included, "Do not be afraid." "Do not be afraid," is written in the Bible 365 times, once for every day of the year—proof to me that humankind has for a very long time needed a reminder to take risks and trust someone or something.

Towards the end of the sermon, Dad told the story of an exchange between himself and Major Girdlestone during a training exercise at Ft Sill in the winter of 1971. Major Girdlestone was the gunnery instructor of Field Artillery Training. One afternoon Dad's team was being evaluated on their ability to direct fire. The target was a personnel carrier. The proper process was to call fire on the target then adjust the fire to bracket it. The view was particularly difficult because there were several small hills which made observation a challenge. The first round fell short. Dad gave the correction, "Add 200!" which he thought would put the round on the far side of the target. It fell short. He gave another correction, "Add 200!" Still short. He was about to give a third order to, 'Add 200!' when the major shouted, "Hold!"

Looking my dad in the eye he said, "Be bold, lieutenant!"

Dad shouted, "Add 1,000!"

Dad would go on to say that during their marriage he and my mom would say to one another, "Be Bold," when they needed to assure or remind or encourage one another to take a risk, or to stay the course, to be strong.

He ended his sermon saying, "Be Bold. Do not be afraid. Have joy and gratitude and don't make decisions based on fear." Sitting in the pew on this particular Sunday, I needed this call to be brave. I vowed to be bold. I vowed to go in increments of 2,000 instead of 200. I asked myself, "Where am I saying no when I should be saying yes? Where am I saying yes when I should be saying no? Where am I lacking courage? Where am I coming up short?" Listening to my gut in this place of rediscovering my "so what" I realized there was so much more I could do, right where I was.

WE OFTEN THINK we need to change something to find meaning and purpose, that meaning and purpose are somewhere "over there." Maybe you tell yourself you don't have time. You don't need examples; you know the dizziness of inner-speak, spending most of your time in the past and in the future. There's the option to plop down and take in what's here, right now. If you want your time to be more meaningful, slow down and find the meaning where you are. The meters you have to go, the distance, is usually right inside of you.

Getting over my "so-what" hump hinged in part on letting go of so much control within my work. In my day-in day-out work persona I was doing deep listening and dedicated work execution. I am a get-things-done kind of gal. To push myself back into purpose, I knew it was time for me to come out from behind my desk and lead. Facing my fear of letting go was a key aspect of scaling a team and building outward. I remember hearing someone say in my early days of parenting, "I gave you life so you can live it." It was in relation to how we can see our own lives separate from our children's—remembering it's their life to live. This notion came back to me: I don't need to relive my early career through you, I hired you to do a job so you can do it. And there are much better ways of doing things now, technology has changed, perspectives. I used to smoke cigarettes at my desk. We've come a long way.

It was time to let go of the reins. When I did there was space for me to do the things I'm now best at: sharing stories, gaining buy-in, teaching, encouraging and making decisions.

One of the things I'm often called to do at work is help others to access their courage. Getting courageous and trusting one's voice starts by understanding who you want to be when you show up. One way to do this is to create the state from which you want to show up. In our vast library of lived experience we have stored memories of what it feels like to be in a rainbow of different emotions. You may be surprised at how quickly and easily you can tap into them. Do you want to go into this meeting and be curious or brave, direct or humble? Fill in the blank.

Take a minute here, imagine a time in the past week when you felt joyful. Hopefully the inquiry alone brought a smile to your face. Close your eyes, and put yourself back in that place. What were you wearing? Who was with you? What do you see? Listen for the voices around you—were there any smells that bring that time and place right back into your senses?

Once you fix the occasion in your mind it only takes a few seconds. Sit with it a moment longer. Can you feel it again, there with you? Imagine if you could bottle that feeling up and when you need a whiff you could uncork the bottle and infuse a bit of joy into whatever you're about to do.

Well, you can—you just did. (I hope).

The amazing thing is that you can replicate this practice to create any state of mind you'd like. You can take a minute before your next meeting, before sitting down to dinner with friends, before tackling a tough conversation, to think about who you want to be in this interaction. Think of a time when you were courageous. Or curious. Or when you felt safe. Or funny. You have access to all of those states of being, already logged in your mind. Creating a state of mind so you're showing up for whatever you're called to do with courage, balance, curiosity, sincerity—the ability to be fully present. This doesn't happen overnight and it does take practice. In my experience, once you see the difference it makes even once, it becomes easier and easier to remember to set an intention and to create a state of being that will best suit whatever situation you're heading into.

My son and I were sitting on the couch watching television when he was around five or six years old. A Snickers commercial came on and the Snickers marketing campaign one-liner was, and I think still is, "Because you're not you when you're hungry."

My son looked over at me as serious as a sermon on Easter and said, "That's so true!"

If you're not you when you're hungry, when are you, you?

In Dad's sermon, Major Girdlestone's call to "Be Bold" was about going further, firing farther and acting with decisiveness.

What echoed for me was the opposite. For me it was about holding back. It was about reining in my fear, letting go of control and trusting my voice. Sometimes being bold means stepping back and getting grounded in one's strength before taking action.

One message. Multiple uses.

Where are you lacking courage? Where are you coming up short? How will you make up the distance?

Be Bold.

Be Bold, Lieutenant!

Jennifer Leslie

Jennifer Leslie is a human resources executive, writer, and meditation teacher who revels in empowering others to thrive. She is an alumna of the InnerMBA program and a neurolinguistic programming coach practitioner. Jennifer resides in Jersey City, New Jersey, with her husband, who good-naturedly requests that she refrain from practicing her hocus-pocus on him.

THREE

Integrating the Moments of Mystical Self-Surrender

Aimee Serene

After years in the fast-paced corporate world a unique opportunity found me. Due to my unique blend of business operations and background in the healing arts I was scouted to manage a holistic center. The role promised not just a job but a transformative journey.

At this center, where we guided clients into deep states of meditation, my life took an unexpected turn. One of our clients, a woman with a delicate radiance that seemed out of place in this tumultuous world, presented an invitation that changed the course of my life. We made plans to travel together to a retreat and for two weeks before our departure she was fervently connecting me with people at our destination, ensuring every detail was perfect. Her life was a series of journeys, always in motion.

Then just two days before our trip, a call shattered my world. One of our mutual friends informed me that the woman had died by suicide. With swollen eyes I boarded the plane to an unknown destination and an imaginary future yet to unfold. My suitcase was full of clothes and tears.

For years I had searched for answers from a place of fear and felt a longing deep inside for the questions I couldn't yet articulate. There was an inexplicable pull towards something I couldn't see or understand; my intuition was urging me to listen closely. Unknown parts of myself needed attention and I was being guided down a path of growth and healing and of expanding my understanding of consciousness.

One of the steps on my journey led me to a sacred place and to the loving soul who cares for this special land, who I now call The Farmer—a person who would forever change my life.

At the airport The Farmer greeted me and together we mourned the loss of our friend. We didn't truly know the depth of pain she was in; her life ended too soon. I realized too that I didn't know the depth of *my* pain and was afraid of what I would learn on the path of healing that has become my life's work.

I watched the trees pass in a blur as we drove up into the countryside and entered a hidden meadow, nestled in the valley. I was present in a sacred place, stewarded by a stream, with my new friend, The Farmer, the sweetest man I have met in this lifetime. He serves the world in a good way, and I love him for it. He is a tender soul who for over sixty years has contributed to the consciousness revolution in extraordinary ways.

Stepping out of the car a profound sense of safety enveloped me, a deeply comforting sensation in an unfamiliar space. My arrival was marked by swirling energy, from sadness and fear of the unknown. Exhausted, I felt the void of my friend's absence, realizing the first lesson: your journey is yours alone, yet you are never truly alone. The land seemed to welcome me, its ancient energy vibrating through my body with each step I took. This place tickled my senses with its tall valley walls, the whispers of the stream, the song of the birds, the stillness in the space between sounds. Walking towards the cabin that would become my retreat for the next week, I felt the sting of tears that flowed down my cheeks.

As I closed the door behind me I fell to the floor and the floodgate of sadness opened, washing over me with waves of grief, fear, and longing. I laid down and sank into the soft bed, took a few deep breaths and closed my eyes. The blanket, damp from the tropical humidity, moistened my skin and sent chills up my arms as the breeze blew through the open windows, bringing with it the soft rustle of the leaves in the trees. I whispered prayers back to the wind, asking to be free of the pain I had carried for so long. The steady flow of the stream that carved its path in search of the sea created an ambient soundscape that suddenly became sharp and clear.

Crying tears for myself, for my lost friend, and for all of the pain I saw in the world around me, I surrendered and exhaled, attempting to quiet my mind. The birds suddenly stopped chirping and the sound of the stream faded away to silence.

That was when the shift occurred—my racing mind became still. I slipped into the space between dreams and opened my eyes wide with curiosity. The weight of my body and sadness were no longer with me, the bed and the cabin no longer existed.

I found myself on an island, standing at the top of a mountain. I gazed past the sea to the horizon, feeling its vastness stretch out before me. Wind blowing from all directions, it felt like I was in a place that existed outside of time. Tall grass blowing in golden waves across the mountaintop meadow, softly breathing and whispering the wisdom of the Earth to any ears attuned to hear her. I stood touching the tips of tall blades that reached up to meet my fingertips as though greeting old friends. This was just the beginning of a beautiful invitation.

I was transported to a different space, where moments seemed to stretch for hours. I raced across the mountaintop as fast as the wind into a world of expansive experiences that permeated all of my senses with their wisdom. Lessons of courage, trust, and compassion enveloped me on the mountain as a canyon in the distance called me to explore its depths, and invited me to dive in. I jumped into the darkness and fell, with arms wide like open wings. Turning my body to gaze up, I watched the view of the sky get smaller as the walls of the canyon grew taller as they enveloped me in their firm silence—not even the sound of the wind existed as I slipped into the unknown abyss of myself. As I fell I thought, "What if I never come back?" and tears fell with me for the radiant soul that I missed, knowing she fell too far and couldn't return.

Traversing the mountaintop of introspection, I was greeted by moments of awe and wonder, where time seemed to stand still and the boundaries of reality dissolved. In the depths of my being I encountered a profound sense of unity and reverence for the interconnectedness of all things. I feel this like an ancestral story that flows through my body like waves and pours out of my eyes as saltwater that joins the sea of gratitude in my heart. **Feeling, sensing, and knowing can be a great weight to bear, something important to know on the path of becoming self-aware.**

Deep in that spectacular meditation, I left as quickly as I arrived: in the blink of an eye. I heard The Farmer's call in the distance, like a birdsong, calling me back to the cabin in the jungle valley. With a deep breath I felt myself push up and out, in my bed once more. My heart sank and a wave of sadness washed over me, knowing that I might never see that place again. The weight of my emotions felt heavy once more. The Farmer knocked at the door and his eyes looked into mine. He knew where I had been and we both knew that was my invitation to something deeper.

This meditation was one of my ways in. The awe. The fear. The release. *The waves of mystical self-surrender.* My life has been dedicated to integrating the lessons that come through this practice of self-awareness. When I close my eyes I can still find myself in that beautiful moment of pure presence, where I felt weightless and free from fear. When distance separates me from that memory and my heart longs to return, I am reminded of my humanity and the enduring sanctuary within myself that transcends the confines of linear reality.

OUR INNER WORLD IS LIMITLESS, uniquely experienced through our eyes and hearts, yet infinitely interconnected. Inside us, there is no "right side up." In a world where people are hurting deeply, our search for salvation and healing becomes paramount. My experience of awe gifted to me from that mountaintop medicine have left me shimmering from my moments of mystical self-surrender, each taking years to integrate and understand as I stepped back into the office and Monday morning meetings.

Yet, amidst the yearning for more in my consciousness exploration journeys, I recognize the potential to be overwhelmed by these experiences, sometimes leading to severe depression when left unsupported. Is this what I saw in my lost radiant friend who chased retreats and experiences that never allowed her to integrate? A feeling too overwhelming to bear?

Now I hold space for those who feel deeply, acknowledging the process of unfolding self-awareness and the power of integration. Looking back I wish I had been more attuned to her struggles, more aware of the inner turmoil she concealed. She was a seeker, constantly retreating from the chaos of the world in search of solace. If only I had known her better maybe I could have helped her find the support she desperately needed.

I saw so much of her in myself, and that was a catalyst for the work I do as an Integration Coach, lovingly walking with people through their process of introspection in ways I wish I had been supported earlier on my journey. Asking for, and receiving support, is a gift of self-compassion as we embrace and navigate the depths of emotion with profound reverence.

Trusting so implicitly that I could shape my reality in this meditation experience was a profound lesson in believing in myself. I have re-read the reflection that I captured countless times over the years, and when I close my eyes every single moment is as clear as though it were yesterday, though I can never show it to anyone else. No one else will visit my mountain, or feel the ground, the grass, and the wind of the places that I have seen. They will instead visit their own sacred space within themselves.

. . .

PATIENCE HAS ALSO BEEN AN ENDURING lesson. We don't have to try to learn everything all at once, self-awareness is a lifelong practice, and I believe that healing and consciousness-expansion can span many lifetimes. In my experience, when I am presented with the next layer of wounds, fears, or lessons it is because those parts of myself feel safe enough to reveal themselves. This has taken time and consistent trust-building with every facet of my internal system. Only then does the inner world present itself to me on the altar of love, ready to allow the pain of the past to heal and transform.

It takes courage to look within. On this path, we encounter infinite paths to a divine place—sometimes through seemingly simple day-to-day moments. Other times, through enormous experiences fraught with overwhelming grandiosity, as we grapple with the enormity and complexity of emotion, questions emerge. Integration becomes vital, and allows us to assimilate the lessons and interpret the signals sent by our experiences each day. How do I bring that wisdom back out, and who am I, with this newfound knowledge and understanding? How do I show up in the world differently?

In these times, many are searching for a place of peace—a quiet space that holds the serenity and wisdom of our inner guidance. This journey of becoming self-aware involves numerous paths, each as distinct as the individual taking it. There are countless ways to embark on this journey, utilizing combinations of techniques and tools that resonate personally. For some this involves integrating daily practices into their lives, for others immersive experiences create a container for deep healing, illuminating the path to intuition and creativity.

The journey inward is not one of isolation, but of connection—a journey that shapes not only who we are, but how we show up in the world. In the sacred spaces of self-exploration we discover the courage to lead from the inside out—to navigate the complexities of existence with humility and grace. As we embrace the fullness of our being we become beacons of light, guiding others on their own journey of self-discovery and transformation.

Our capacity to connect with others is limited only by the depth

Integrating the Moments of Mystical Self-Surrender

of our connection with ourselves. So let us embark on this journey together, with hearts open and minds willing, knowing that the path to leadership begins within. For it is only by embracing and integrating our own truth that we can truly inspire others to do the same.

AIMEE SERENE

Aimee Serene

Aimee Serene is the founder of Serene Integration and a certified coach with fifteen years of experience in business operations and retreat management. She specializes in plant medicine integration and utilizes her background in a wide range of healing modalities to support changemakers in their transformative journeys. Aimee's unique approach bridges the corporate and cosmic realms, fostering holistic personal and professional growth. Co-founder and Chief Program Officer of Changing Work, Aimee resides in Northern California with her husband and two dogs, Ben and Rose.

FOUR

Beyond Myself

Rachael O'Meara

It was early October 2011 and the autumn air was crisp in San Francisco. I was thirty-nine years old and excited for the weekend ahead. I had returned to Google the month before after a three-month hiatus, or pause, to untangle myself from burnout and over-thinking about what lay ahead in my career. For the first time in my life I was knee-deep in personal growth books and my head was swimming with ideas on how to live my life from this new vantage point.

I was excited about leading a day-long bike tour in Napa, a new side-hustle. While I was prepping my bike and laying my clothes out for my trip, I reminded myself of what I recently learned from watching Oprah.

"Surrender to what you no longer want to worry about, and hand it over to God."

Then I heard myself mumble out loud, as though my thoughts had won a wrestling match against my vocal cords, "OK Jesus. I hereby surrender to you. I hand my worries fully over to you. I am done worrying!"

I didn't think much of it but I meant it. I finished my prep, pumped my bike tires, and slithered into bed excited to bike.

I woke up to a loud buzzing as the digital alarm clock flashed 5:15a.m. There was an unusual, almost eerie quiet in the stillness enveloping me. It was almost tangible. I realized I had no thoughts. This was in stark contrast to my typical mental monologue, noticeably absent, and which sounded more like a drill-sergeant ordering me around. Where was she?

I swung my feet out of bed and felt the cold wood floor. Every sensation was amplified. Sounds were louder. My vision was sharper. I went about my business, gathered my bike, and drove out of the garage in my SUV. Still no drill-sergeant voice. I shockingly had no judgements to rattle off. I couldn't even think of anything to say in the vacuum of silence in which I found myself. I had no words—no thoughts—to explain this new state. There were no other witnesses. Was I going insane?

I drove in awe across the Golden Gate Bridge. I felt connected to the road underneath my feet as my car bounced over the potholes on the highway. The night sky twinkled in my tinted windows. The sunrise painted fiery red and orange hues across the Pacific. I felt safe, peaceful and serene. Still no thoughts. Somehow I had flipped a mental switch that stopped not just one but *all* my thoughts. Only my heightened awareness and sensory perception remained. Could it be that what Oprah had advised had worked, and God had heard my prayer?

After an hour I arrived at my destination. I looked to my left and was greeted by a double rainbow. It felt like a wink from the heavens reminding me, "Yes, you are one with us! We see you, and welcome!"

Then the tears came. My cold, dry cheeks were now wet and soaking up the inexplicable wonder I felt pouring out of me. Immense gratitude washed over me as I walked through the terracotta vineyard and earthy soils to the bike shack. I was seeing things as if for the first time in my life, and I was inside some kind of kaleidoscope. Colors popped and were luminous and brighter. Ordinary things like rocks, trees, and cars had a luminous quality as if I hadn't ever seen one quite like it before, calling out for my attention.

My morning continued in this fashion. I felt paralyzed from the inside out knowing my inner world had been seismically rocked. Whatever was unfolding, I didn't completely understand it.

On the bike tour I carried on conversations and drove the support van without missing a beat. I pondered, "Can they tell what's happening to me!?" Others had no clue. I was the only one. There was an inner knowing that I was connected to all living things. I felt an invisible umbilical cord directly connecting me to an unseen force—call it God, Universe, or whatever—and it was holding me perfectly in place, connected to all things seen and unseen around me.

I found myself at our lunch stop. The winery, like everything I encountered that day, was breathtaking. The al fresco patio shimmered with jewel-toned tiles and opulent marble tables as I went through the motions of setting up lunch. I stared up at the hundred-foot poplar trees that surrounded the property. They whispered, "Hello!" Their leaves were glimmering in the streaks of sunlight.

I stared up in disbelief. These giant, stunning trees were like guardians, glowing and changing color, like a sequined spectacle of the double rainbow earlier that day. They breathed and swayed as they merged with my breathing and being. I felt the trees feeling me feeling them. They continued speaking but not through words. There was a pulsing and a presence I felt as they collectively confirmed, "We welcome you to this new way of being, Rachael. We are so glad you are here. Yes, this is real. We love you. Yes, this is the work of God."

I was beyond myself, hanging with God in this unexpected gift. It was as if God sent his private jet to pick me up, take me on a day tour, then drop me off effortlessly. I felt a profound sense of wholeness and the tears returned. I was in a whirlwind of sublime overload yet calm and comforted. I had an unexplainable knowing that I was not alone. It didn't have words, but rather a presence and love that was pouring into me faster than I knew what to do with.

I felt like I had unlocked the secrets of the universe. We were all a part of a greater plan. I knew I would never feel alone or separate again, and I was exactly where I was supposed to be. I felt the universe's heartbeat in sync with mine, expanding and connecting. I tapped into my deep, generative aliveness that was bound not just within myself but was also in everything else. My inner drill-sergeant voice was still long gone with no signs of returning. Instead, hundred-year-old trees were exchanging vibes with me.

I churned over how fortunate I felt. How did I so easily get this gift of the secrets of the universe? I didn't get cancer or some rare disease that made me question everything. I had no close calls with death. Instead, this gift fell softly and ever so gently like a feather finally finding gravity. It was mine to relish and to decide what to do with from here.

Since that fateful day, my life plotted a new trajectory. I felt like I had proof that each of us is connected in ways far beyond our physical bodies.

TODAY, experiencing life beyond my physical self continues to fuel my energy in ways I couldn't previously imagine. If I feel tired or burned out I remember how I felt the day I went beyond myself in Napa. Each of us can manage our energy knowing this, and when we do, our world can transform as leaders, humans, and ambassadors of what's possible.

We are more connected to ourselves, and as a result, to others. We can be less stressed and more purposeful in everything we do. When we say yes to managing our energy and making it our top priority—noticing how we feel, expressing ourselves, asking for support, remembering we are part of something bigger—we tap into unlimited energy and into resources beyond ourselves. This can include our surroundings: the ground, the sky, or whatever is in "the field" around us.

When we do this our to-dos aren't the be-all-end-all that they once were. We can feel more at ease. We can relax knowing the world won't stop turning if we don't finish sending that last email. Instead, set time aside to pause accordingly. As a result, we are more connected to ourselves, and recognize when we feel sad, depleted, and even joyful. In my case I no longer fear being with myself. I can move towards self-acceptance and redirect the chastising inner drill-sergeant voice anytime I need to.

We can all rely and trust our intuition and instincts more than we realize. When this happens we have infinite energy to draw from and our energy is replenished. It could mean a pause like a walk outside (or a bike ride) where I draw up energy from the ground, or down from the sky. It could be a mindful breath, journaling to process my day, or naming a feeling I have. I can send my anger into the ground down through my feet. I can remember what I'm grateful for, and thus conjure up feelings of pure joy that wouldn't otherwise exist. Energy is our aliveness, and we can choose to generate it, avoid it, or dampen it down.

There is not a day where I don't take my energy for granted, and thank God for my aliveness, flow, and self that I discovered on that fateful Napa day. To manage this energy and ensure I feel resourced, confident and calm, I created a three-word mantra to share: **Live Love Lead**. If we orient to these three things every day we can feel more alive, prioritize love, and lead with deep purpose and intention.

Live. Your energy is your life force, and is critical to showing up to live fully—no matter what is on your agenda or how your day is unfolding. Your energy is limitless, and your aliveness directs it. It can also be contained at the same time. To live is to fully show up for yourself, and dial up your aliveness so you feel at your best, fulfilled, and fired up for what excites you or what you choose to create in your day.

When you choose not to direct your energy, you are not as intentional and less effective. It's easier to be more scattered in thoughts, feelings, and behavior. We can flow more in a state that feels intuitive, guided, and real. This is your inner leader, knowing what's best and how to navigate what's ahead. You know you are not alone as you forge forward in your to-dos and moments of insight that sprinkle your day. This means you trust yourself, and your energy.

You may forget this, and it's okay to not be perfect every day. In fact, you may have a terrible day, but it doesn't define you. Deep down, you realize you can connect and re-center to align as you dip into the nourishment and replenishment that's always available. It feels empowering, as if this higher power is always holding you by the hand, nudging you to live what's next and providing a security blanket of feeling safe and supported.

Love. Love all there is to love in your life. Acknowledge the little things every day and practice gratitude. When we're grateful for what we have, we are sending a signal to ourselves and the universe that we are happy for what is working well, and that we are ready for more if and when we desire. Your energy can be amplified through love and your heart, and it is one of the greatest strengths each of us has.

Lead. Each of us are here to lead the life that is uniquely and specifically yours—professionally and personally. Friends, we are not alone, operating as solo separate humans, even though it may often feel like that. Like I discovered in Napa, we are all interconnected, supported by the universe, and here to serve and learn more lessons than we know. Your assignment is to learn this in your unique way, like I did. When we pause and listen to the inner leader who knows what's best and how to navigate what's ahead, it's then that we can lead in brilliant and purposeful ways.

You can show up brighter and bolder than you would otherwise, and trust yourself and what's unfolding—beyond yourself.

Rachael O'Meara

RACHAEL O'MEARA, MBA, MA, ACC is an executive coach who helps successful leaders learn proven tools and strategies to thrive as leaders. Her thirteen years at Google has helped her keep a finger on the pulse of what it takes to be a strong leader in her private practice and as co-founder of SIC Venture Studio. Her first book 'Pause' was a top business book focused on careers. She's been featured in New York Times, WSJ.com, Harvard Business Review, and on the TEDx stage.

FIVE

Bigger: Accessing the Wisdom of the Expanded Self

Lori Schwanbeck

The sun was climbing high in the blue sky in the Joshua Tree desert as I found myself unable to walk any further. The pain in my ankle was searing and even the part of me that likes to push beyond limits had to admit defeat. We had only been walking about five minutes. I half-heartedly encouraged my partner, Mark, to keep exploring—telling him that I would be okay waiting on one of the massive boulders. Perhaps more than feeling limited myself, I hated thinking I was limiting someone else.

Most of my life I have been exceptionally active and even a near-fatal bicycle accident resulting in a reconstructed ankle, didn't deter me from living fully. Definite adjustments had to be made: flamenco dancing became yoga, running became walking, and getting into the mountains now required a horse. But this time was different. Now, even walking was difficult, and some days impossible. Activities with friends, work trips, and even grocery shopping had suddenly stopped.

Beyond the pain, the logistical challenges, and the canceled client engagements that came with this most recent decrease in mobility, what became most excruciating was my inner life. The dire predictions of doctors seen years ago after the bike accident were spinning me into despair. I was told that at some point far in the future, my reconstructed ankle would likely deteriorate and I'd face multiple surgeries with no guaranteed outcome. But I was reassured that I'd be a little old lady by the time this happened. Even with the limitations, I was told many times how lucky I was to be alive.

Knowing I was on bonus time, with an uncertain future, a wholehearted appreciation for life blossomed in me. Daily I would feel grateful for the activities I could still do along with the facilitation work that took me around the globe. But now everything was different, and I couldn't walk. Was my life of mobility over? At fifty-five had I reached old lady status?

My years of teaching mindfulness and emotional intelligence in organizations had been a wonderful way for me to reinforce the skills that I (now?) used daily to focus attention and cultivate emotional well-being. After my accident, despite the injuries, I was flourishing, feeling purposeful in my work as I shared practices that helped me, and others, manage stress, create emotional balance, and manage reactivity. Armed with the neuroscience that validates the effect of attention training on body, brain, and behavior—and buoyed by my own personal experience of cultivating a growth mindset amidst challenges—I felt well-used in teaching resilience skills. I taught the importance of recognizing when one is stuck in pessimism, where setbacks are seen as personal, pervasive, and permanent, and how to shift into a more balanced mindset that helps one see challenges less catastrophically. This worked when the setback was handling the sting of difficult feedback or having project proposals rejected. It even worked when I lost a significant amount of money in an investment.

The mental training practices I taught to others, I used myself.

And they worked… until they didn't.

With my most recent decline in mobility, I spiraled into catastrophic, negative thinking. I was aware of it but trying to shift out of rumination was impossible. Of course, this is *personal*… I must have done something wrong to have fast-tracked myself into old lady status. Of course, this is *pervasive*… it's affecting everything in my life, from work to daily tasks to gathering with friends. Of course this is *permanent*.... There was no solution that guaranteed I'd be able to walk. Being in my body was painful. But being in my head was even worse.

I was missing being able to move and also missed the mindset of optimism that I could so often cultivate regardless of circumstances, the mindset I had so earnestly encouraged others to find. Not only was I immobile and dependent, but I was also a fraud. My life's work was a sham. In Joshua Tree alone with my ruminating mind, watching Mark as he went on hiking while I sat, it hit me.

I wasn't alone, really. I was surrounded by life—animals, plants, and rocks—all of which had evolved by learning to survive in challenging circumstances. Feeling the presence of the wider world beyond my own small self, I recalled the personal practice that along with mindfulness, also informs my life. It is a practice that I rarely bring into my corporate training as I find it difficult to translate into business language and lack the requisite neuroscience to validate it. This is a practice that is not about working with the *contents* of the mind, but about *dissolving* the personal mind altogether and merging with a bigger mind.

When wisdom couldn't be found in my own head, I turned to guidance from life around me. The ancient, deep-time wisdom found in nature.

As I sat on the rocks, I sensed the presence of life that was older and vaster than my own. The intelligence of nature began speaking through the rocks. To the part of me feeling grief my limited mobility would cause me to miss out on experiencing life personally and professionally, the rocks said: "Wait a minute sister! Look at us. We are sedentary and of course we still experience life! We don't chase after experiences; life comes to us. This is your chance to know you are 'enough' and to stop trying to prove yourself. Less seeking and more savoring."

The wisdom from the rocks filled five pages in my journal. As I listened and took in their perspective, I felt supported and curious. I felt bigger than the myopic world of self-pity and grief that I had been stuck in.

. . .

LATER THAT EVENING I watched the infinite expanse of desert sky as dusk descended, and the first star of the night began to brightly gleam. To the part of me overwhelmed by uncertainty and fear about what my future held, the newly emerged star said: "I've always been here. The conditions simply had to change for you to see me. Possibility is like that. Clarity will emerge in its own time. Wherever there is uncertainty, there is possibility."

I felt bigger than fear and doubt.

Seeing myself as an expression of the same life that shaped the wizened rocks, I learned humility, curiosity, and acceptance. The vast night sky taught me patience and possibility. By listening to the wider world around me I had become bigger. Or I should say, the self I know myself to be, the one formed around accomplishments, preferences, and ideas of how life should be, became smaller relative to the vastness of life itself. It took the ancient stones, the clear night sky, and the desert landscape sculpted by the inevitability of harsh conditions to right-size my identity and put my personal story into perspective.

WHAT IS A BIGGER SELF?

Paradoxically, it is a self where parts of us get smaller. Our reference points of 'me', 'I', and 'mine', constrained by our biography, resume, and even the contents of our thinking mind—shrink relative to the unbounded self who experiences itself as an interconnected part of the world. It's easy to accept that our bodies are dynamically shaped by nature—our physicality influenced by what we eat, the air we breathe, and the light we are exposed to. Why not include our minds and our hearts, as phenomena that also emerge, evolve, and dynamically interact with nature? Knowing ourselves to be part of something bigger gives us access to perspectives and wisdom gleaned from the collective, including the more-than-human world.

Expanding our sense of self benefits our own lives, and we also become more resourced when responding to other people's lives. We touch into a sense of vastness, a place from which all of life arises:

you, me, this tree, this struggle, this joy. There's more space around it all. Compassion for ourselves and others becomes easier. Facing challenges and having difficult conversations becomes easier. We sense that whatever we are going through isn't personal. We see that all of life is adapting to changing circumstances, some that are pleasant, some that are hard. It's part of the deal. Perspective, compassion, and equanimity are the fruits of sensing our expanded self.

SO HOW DO we access this bigger self?

1. Acknowledge. The first step is knowing when you're stuck. It's recognizing when you've come to the limits of working with the contents of your mind and when it's time to access GPT. No, not the virtual *information* source. Rather, consulting the *wisdom* source found in the organic world which gives us NatureGPT: *Greater Perspective Taking.* There is literally a world of difference. Our minds, opened with curiosity and humility, can then expand as we orient to something outside of ourselves that has co-evolved with the same dynamic conditions that we have. Hint: it's not on(?) a screen.

2. Be Aware. Notice the sense of opening and responsiveness you feel as you become aware of what you experience in the present moment. What happens in the mind in the presence of a still, clear lake? What is touched in you as you see a golden sunrise crest over a mountain? What happens in your belly as you observe the industriousness of a bird building her nest? These responses are indications you are becoming permeable, that the boundary between what is outside and what is inside is beginning to soften. As you feel yourself open, drawn up and out of your thinking mind, your self-awareness becomes bigger.

3. Listen. Once you become attuned to your responsiveness to the broader world, now is the time to listen for wisdom. A spontaneous insight may arise that is relevant to your life, as the desert boulders offered by reassuring me that I would continue to live a full life, even if more sedentary. You can also ask for specific guidance. The response may come in the form of metaphor, mental clarity, a sensation in the body or a movement of the heart. This is GPT in action. As I looked up at the desert sky I held the question: "How will I find a doctor who knows how to help me?" The star said: "You can do this. Wherever there is uncertainty, there is possibility." With this response I felt the anxiety ease. In listening for guidance, you might not get a specific answer as I did from the star. But continuing to hold the question itself creates a sense of curiosity and invites a continual conversation with the wider world.

4. Apply. This is an important step. It can be easy to fall back into the small self and forget or dismiss the embodied insights coming from the expanded self. Creating multi-sensory reminders are helpful as they more readily evoke an embodied remembering. When working on deadlines, take a photograph of the bird nest to remind you of the part of yourself that is industrious and creative. Whenever I feel contracted and afraid for my health, I look at the photo of me sitting on the giant desert boulders, and I recall the feeling of their solid reassurance—am reminded of the possibility of acceptance with my life regardless of conditions. I feel more resourced in facing uncertainty.

ONE OF THE few times I have brought this practice into a business setting, I had the leadership team take their questions to the meadow outside of their office and listen for answers. James, whose co-workers had struggled with his dominant leadership style, wanted to increase his awareness of a dynamic that had become a blind spot for him. While outside, he observed the Scotch Broom, a non-native plant that had taken over. It was bright yellow, getting lots of attention, but choked out opportunities for other plants to grow and so the ecosystem suffered. The bigger world offered a mirror that expanded his self-awareness, enabling him to see the impact his leadership style had on the functioning of the team. He brought back a branch of the plant and put it on his desk to remind him to pause and give more space for others. He became bigger than his own self-importance.

Working with the content of the mind through mindfulness training and emotional intelligence is still useful. In a world where distractions are rampant and our nervous systems are constantly activated, we need to train our attention. As my desert experience invites us to remember, there is a rich world of wisdom accessible as we expand the mind and our sense of self.

Nature is only one way to access our bigger self. Remembering that you are part of a long lineage of people who have survived and even thrived through challenges, and drawing on the resources and values passed through your ancestors, is another way. Being moved by awe and feeling the sense of being touched beyond your thinking mind, is another. Connecting to a purpose or a spiritual practice, is you getting bigger. Acts of compassion motivated by a sense of common humanity is also you getting bigger.

How do you get bigger, and what becomes possible as you feel your expanded self?

Lori Schwanbeck

~

LORI SCHWANBECK is a psychotherapist, mindfulness teacher, program designer and facilitator in organizations worldwide. Her work weaves together the practicality of neuroscience-backed emotional intelligence skills, embodiment practices and positive psychology, all infused with the wisdom of nature. Lori founded Mindfulness Therapy Associates and is also core faculty at the Search Inside Yourself Leadership Institute, the Modern Elder Academy, Esalen Institute, Humanize, and Awake in the Wild. Her joy is cultivating aliveness and whole-hearted connection.

Embracing Your Change

SIX

What Inmates Can Teach Us About Vulnerability

Jeff Jacobs

Robert wanted to be vulnerable but it could cost him his life. Breathing accelerated and unable to stop his tears, he bit his lip and pulled his blue ski cap down to obscure his eyes. The cap matched the denim shirt and pants which were standard issue for the "men in blue." This was when Robert confessed to me the crime which placed him in "Charlie Yard" of a maximum-security prison twenty long years ago. He quickly wiped his eyes and nose with the oversized sleeves of his shirt. I watched his glance dart around the locked gymnasium to make sure he wasn't seen. It took three full days for our relationship to build to this point. Not much time under normal circumstances, but an eternity for someone who hasn't had a visitor or received a piece of mail for years. Robert was clear: any sign of weakness could, and likely would, be used against him by his fellow inmates, as well as by the prison guards.

I have probably met over a hundred inmates since starting my participation in Prison Ministry, and yet this moment with Robert stands out to me more than most. We all put on façades at different moments in our lives, to posture or to save face, but Robert's façade of strength and bravado was literally for his physical safety. And yet he trusted me enough to embrace the vulnerability of expressing himself. To be clear, this wasn't about me. Thirty other volunteers around the prison were having their own experiences with these men. This was about establishing a personal relationship, and a demonstration of the power of trust and safety, and our hunger for vulnerability.

We choose to come to "Charlie Yard" because it houses the most severe offenders in this prison. These are the "shot callers" who set the tone for everyone else. If we can influence the culture with these men, they will then influence the culture throughout the institution of close to three thousand men. *They are the leaders.*

I AM WELL into my third decade as a human resources professional, the last ten years of which I have spent working with executives and senior leadership teams as a coach, consultant, and facilitator.

Over my career, I have had numerous experiences with C-level executives. I, and teams I have led, have been recognized with awards from executives; I have also been ushered out of their offices and even out of companies. I have had my input avoided and ignored, and I have been invited into boardrooms and onto corporate jets. At one time in my career I was told I didn't have the necessary influence to work with executives. At several other points, I was flown around the world to offer my input and support for key initiatives. I have experienced one chief executive officer scream insults and throw things in his office, and another share his personal performance review so everyone was aware and could help him with his strengths and opportunities. I worked with one C-level executive who avoided her extended team in favor of just interacting with her direct reports, and another who walked the halls daily to connect with as many different employees as possible.

I offer these examples to illustrate that just like the "shot callers" of Charlie Yard, the behavior of these executives influenced the cultures of the organizations they were leading, *and* my behavior with them influenced my own success and failure along the way.

What Inmates Can Teach Us About Vulnerability

Let me be explicit. At the heart of conscious business practices is the requirement to develop and foster a safe and trusting work environment. It means I feel comfortable discussing the unique "superpowers" which I bring to my work, as well as my opportunity areas. If I am to grow and develop, I must feel safe to acknowledge that I have room to grow and develop. A safe and trusting work environment means I am free to speak up honestly and authentically. This openness not only enhances engagement, loyalty, collaboration, and innovation, it also enables us to bring all the elephants into the room and address them because we feel comfortable doing so. It enables us to be vulnerable.

I don't anticipate that anyone is going to argue the value of developing and fostering a safe and trusting work environment where people can be vulnerable. The challenge is that doing so requires us to model vulnerability ourselves.

Why is this so difficult? Let's go back to some of my less-than-positive executive experiences.

Why did I have my input avoided and ignored?

Why was I told at one point that I didn't have the necessary influence to work with executives?

Why did I lose a job at a company I adored?

While there are several contributing factors, a critical one was my reluctance to be vulnerable. As an HR professional I had taught and even preached the value of having a growth mindset, of regularly soliciting and acting on feedback, of acknowledging weaknesses and asking for help. But I wasn't practicing what I was preaching. This wasn't intentional on my part; it was a blind spot. I didn't see it. I didn't recognize it. Years of angry reflection after losing a job I enjoyed at a company that worked hard to foster safety and trust finally gelled into the realization that I had to take some responsibility.

It was easy and rewarding to play the victim and complain about not getting sufficient guidance and of being set up to fail. Passive aggressive gossiping and complaining felt good and it wasn't tough to find an audience. Explaining why feedback was wrong and rationalizing that people just didn't understand put a self-imposed ceiling on my success. The alternative of accepting critical feedback and asking for help felt as though it would cause irreparable harm to my brand and put an immediate halt to my career.

I am clearly not alone in this mindset. One study found that 68% of CEOs feared they would lose respect if they showed empathy in the workplace.[1] We're not even talking about personal vulnerability here, we're talking about empathy for others. For many of us a sharp line exists between our personal and professional lives, between the serious professional we feel we need to be at work and the person we are with family and friends.

The analogies between my professional work and my prison work consistently surprise me. Yes, my "professional" skills help me manage conversations with the "men in blue." But what I didn't expect was how much the "men in blue" would teach me about the professional world. Vulnerability in prison can literally be a matter of life and death. The equivalent in the corporate world is our perceived credibility, our professional brand.

THE BEST THING we can do to influence a culture of trust, safety, and vulnerability is to model vulnerability ourselves. When we model vulnerability, we implicitly give permission to others to do the same. But some of us don't have that privilege. Some of us don't work in cultures which embrace that degree of authenticity. While the goal would be to find a safe and trusting culture in which you can be more of your "true self," some of us don't have the privilege of changing roles, bosses, or organizations any more than inmates have the privilege of changing cell blocks.

This got me to thinking. What did we do to make inmates in a maximum-security prison feel safe enough to express themselves as they hadn't done for years, when the potential cost to their physical and emotional well-being could be so great? And whatever we did, might it be transferable to a work world which aspires to create environments where individuals can "bring their whole selves to work?" It couldn't be that complicated, as we had earned their trust in less than three days. Or could it?

Vulnerability isn't binary. We aren't either vulnerable or not vulnerable. As with many things, vulnerability operates on a spectrum. Whether you are a leader of an organization, a manager of a team, or an individual contributor, you can serve as a change agent to influence your environment. I found the steps to be simple, but not easy. Here are some lessons I learned from my experience with the "men in blue":

Invest time. One inmate told me that I was the first "normal" person he had spoken with in twenty years. You can't establish trust if you don't make time—not just time to catch up on to-dos and deliverables, but time to discuss how someone is doing, what they are thinking and how they are feeling. Don't cancel and move 1:1s. Invest in hallway conversations. We are all busy on our day-to-day deliverables, but we need to invest time in building relationships along the way.

Don't judge. We didn't need to label the men of "Charlie Yard." Their labels were already firmly applied. We didn't deny their situations but didn't belabor them either. We treated them with respect as individuals who were more than the products of their past deeds. For efficiency we commonly judge and label individuals based on limited interactions. I have been quick to label and judge others at different times during my career. Not only were my judgments on many occasions proven wrong, but I also found myself on the receiving end of some of those labels and judgments—strong motivation to look at people differently and consider whether we are giving people the space (and guidance) to change and grow.

Listen. Most of us are familiar with "active listening skills"—maintaining eye contact, encouraging the speaker with a nod or expression which demonstrates that you are following along, reframing, or repeating what you are hearing, etc. Active listening and follow-up questions take time, but they generate insights and open-mindedness not typically encountered when you rehearse your next thought while the other person is still speaking.

Seek to understand. When presented with an opinion, ask follow-up questions to understand the origin of the belief and its strength of conviction. What experiences have led to that point of view? Encourage conversation around the table and around the room.

Model receptivity. As part of their roles, people managers are expected to provide feedback. One of the best ways of modeling and encouraging vulnerability and establishing a "culture of feedback" is simply to ask for feedback yourself. Ask your manager, yes—but also ask your peers and definitely ask your employees. Not only will they be more likely to ask themselves, but they will also be more receptive and honest in your subsequent conversations.

Encourage and appreciate participation. We recognize and show appreciation when our "men in blue" share with the group, often with a simple, "thank you for sharing." In a business context, encouraging "virtual" attendees to chime in, or allowing extra "processing" time on a topic can make a huge difference.

THE MOST COMMON question that I get regarding prison ministry is whether I feel scared walking through the four locked sally port gates at the prison and hearing those doors lock behind me as I come to stand in a concrete gymnasium with more than thirty maximum-security inmates. The answer is no.

We provide these men with a little window of vulnerability so that they can enjoy some normalcy and be reminded that they are human beings who are valued despite the most heinous crimes. We create a small safe, trusting, and vulnerable environment within the broader confines of an institution which is anything but.

Robert's mistake was huge and life-changing. But by acknowledging it, and by accepting the pain of ownership and responsibility, he modeled greater strength and self-compassion in service to his personal growth than he did when he committed the crime twenty years earlier. Since all participants are on similar journeys, they start to have more meaningful and heartfelt conversations than they would otherwise, and they form bonds not previously available to them. Races literally separated by painted lines out on the yard come together, share, and even embrace. The guards, chaplains and even the warden note the difference in the men, across the yard, and throughout the prison. Recidivism studies reinforce the point.

One must ask, if we see progress here, what is to keep us from making progress anywhere?

Jeff Jacobs

~

For over thirty years **JEFF JACOBS** has held a broad range of Human Resources leadership roles, mostly with Adobe, Intuit, and Juniper Networks, all culminating in his passion for and success in executive coaching, consulting, and facilitation. Outside of work, Jeff is married to his college sweetheart, is a proud father to two amazing sons, a non-profit board member, a mental health advocate, a perpetual student of compassion and mindfulness, and a participant in retreat(s), music, and of course, prison ministry.

---

1. BusinesSolver. *State of Workplace Empathy Study.* Author: 2023. https://www.businessolver.com/workplace-empathy/.

SEVEN

Leveraging Self-Awareness for Career Impact

Anna Oakes

They moved my desk to HR. Was this punishment? One minute I'm chatting up the CEO at an after-work event, sharing ideas about our growth plans, and the next thing I know I have a new seat. And a new job. In HR.

Wait, I thought to myself. *I know nothing about HR.*

I was panicking about what I'd gotten myself into. The voices in my head were getting louder so I got quiet. I sat with the idea and meditated, searching for discernment.

As a person who is typically either all in or all out, I struggled to pick a side and drown out the voices. I was desperate to get clear about what *I* wanted and playing it safe had no place here.

Then it happened. An inner knowing. A quiet confidence. An understanding swept over my body. This was my opportunity to grow, learn, and maximize the impact I could have at this company. But, how?

I had watched a few friends start their journeys as entrepreneurs and admired that feeling of freedom and impact in their work and outcomes. They always just seemed to play bigger. Was there a way I could have that too? Could I use my skills in a more targeted way, like they did?

Yes, I decided. Along with the new role I would gift myself another new title: *intra*preneur. I could be effective and creative like an entrepreneur, while choosing to work for someone else.

This was my chance to reclaim ownership of both my talents and my time and to begin to use them strategically for targeted outcomes. Move over entrepreneurs, the impactful intrapreneurs have arrived.

Self-awareness as a career tool

To begin my journey as an impactful intrapreneur, I needed to get real about the skills and experiences I brought to the table and to be prepared to use them in new ways. This understanding of self, what I'm good at and what I'm not so good at, wasn't just the first stage of the journey—it was the journey itself. How could I maximize my impact without being honest about my limitations and my strengths?

Almost twenty years later I'm confident that this commitment to myself was, and remains, the catalyst that helps me excel in roles and advance my career in meaningful ways. But were others experiencing the same thing?

Cornell University conducted a study[1] to see what made CEOs of successful companies so successful. It wasn't strategic thinking. It wasn't empathy for others. Self-awareness was the biggest predictor of CEO success. The father of emotional intelligence, well-known psychologist and author Daniel Goleman[2], believes self-awareness is the cornerstone of emotional intelligence. A Korn Ferry study[3] found that high-earning companies employ people with higher levels of self-awareness.

The fact that high-earning companies specifically seek out employees with high levels of self-awareness speaks volumes about the importance of this trait in the workplace. Companies understand that individuals who possess self-awareness are more likely to be effective communicators, better collaborators, and stronger leaders. These qualities are essential for a thriving and successful organization, which is why self-awareness is increasingly being recognized as a key indicator of potential success.

When individuals are able to truly understand their strengths, weaknesses, and motivations, they are better equipped to make sound decisions and navigate challenging situations. It is not only the foundation of emotional intelligence, but how leadership skills and overall success—both individual and collective—are built.

Putting self-awareness to work

The awareness I was seeking didn't mean there was instant success. I spent the next decade experimenting and continuously auditing what I was good at (and not so good at). I also made a conscious effort to spend time with others who had the same mentality. Even with different roles we could learn from each other. Could I adopt aspects of their efforts for my own journey of impact? Status quo became a thing of the past as I stretched myself and searched for ways to maximize my impact in every role I earned.

I spent the next eleven years in eight different roles at three different companies. Some of the roles I filled weren't new to the organization but many of them were. These new roles were uncharted territory and a direct result of my efforts to operate as an intrapreneur. Whether I was an internal promotion or external hire I made sure to spend time exploring what the role was really meant to do. I engaged the hiring manager in thoughtful conversations about the impact this role could have, not just on my assigned outcomes but on the outcomes of others. Together we dreamed of something more than what they first thought they needed. I was bold in sharing my ideas and asked an obscene amount of questions to make sure we were aligned on the results we would both be driving to.

And if the role wasn't new to the company I still aimed to bring new energy and outcomes to the role, which meant being clear with my leader that I wasn't going to do the job as the last person had done it. I got them excited about my approach and potential outcomes and brought them along on my journey of experimentation. This was a key part of my journey, because historically companies and bosses aren't that great at providing detailed plans on how to really make an impact in a given job or at the company. There's too much left up to interpretation, which is typically incorrect, or involves a lot of low-impact activities. They provide a one- or two-page job description and expect that to be enough to guide the thousands of hours their employees will spend trying to make a difference.

By trying on new behaviors and paying close attention to which efforts produced the results that I wanted, I was able to apply my observations and learnings immediately, adjusting my approach as I went.

The three tenets of an impactful intrapreneur

It's been eighteen years since they moved my desk to HR. Along the way I've failed a lot, but I managed to learn quickly. I've sought out other impactful intrapreneurs and learned there are a few tenets that we all apply in varying degrees. These three tenets, when embodied, will help you maximize your impact and transition well to intrapreneurship.

Be presumptuous. Being presumptuous has gotten a bad rap. I love the Oxford Languages definition of the word: failing to observe the limits of what is permitted or appropriate. Isn't that what entrepreneurs do—push through limits? Why can't I do the same as an impactful intrapreneur? If the way it has always been done is what the company expects, I don't want to work there anyway.

This tenet comes first as it's the one that needs the most practice. You've been groomed as a child and then as an employable adult to take instructions and put them into practice. Rarely were you told to think outside the box or to get creative in what you work on or how you work on it. Managers aren't adequately trained in how to lead a team strategically and tactically, let alone shown how to hire for something different than what they've seen before.

To get there, do what entrepreneurs do. They see a path and work to make it their own in order to find their unique offering that people are willing to pay for. Why should an intrapreneur be any different?

I was presumptuous when I looked beyond the title and job description (how are these the two main data points that companies lead by?) and assumed there was room for interpretation. I was presumptuous when I met my new co-workers and shared my vision for the role. I was presumptuous when I inquired about their impact and how they maximized their impact at a company like this. I was presumptuous when I looked beyond the limitations that were given to me.

Just because I want you to be bold, doesn't mean you can have a laissez-faire attitude when it comes to relationships. Be thoughtful in the way you talk about your work. Push the envelope but ask more questions than you give answers. I found the phrase that helped me put others at ease was, "Here's how I want to maximize my impact at this company." I made it about the results that I would produce and the value that that would bring to the organization, not about how I would go about it or where it would get me. That, after all, should be up to me.

Be likable. I want you to be bold in owning your career and your impact. But if you can't be likable during the process you'll likely fail to bring others along on your journey. And when you have no supporters, followers, or sponsors, your impact will suffer.

You might be rolling your eyes at this advice, but don't shut it out. Much of what made me successful was my ability to tell good stories and manage the change that others were feeling—two things others seemed grateful to receive. Two tools helped me the most: Gallup's CliftonStrengths assessment[4] and learning about change management. The assessment increased my self-awareness and gave me a common language to use when talking about my strengths and weaknesses, and an organized way to talk about applying them to my work. I found that I made others feel safe when I talked confidently about what I was good at and reflected humbly on my areas of weakness. It set the stage for them to reciprocate and many people shared that my approach inspired them to rethink their impact.

I didn't win over everyone. Some thought my efforts were ego-driven and it took me longer to convince them that I was in it to maximize my impact and not to get a title. And while there aren't any risks in being likable there are risks in how you go about getting others to like you. First, the connection has to be genuine. If you have nothing else in common with someone, point to your shared desire to maximize your impact. Remember, impactful intrapreneurs hang with other impactful intrapreneurs and there are plenty of people to share this approach with. Second, use your strengths and their application to your work to win over others. When they see your excitement is genuine they'll likely be open to giving you a chance.

Be curious. Curiosity didn't kill the cat; it helped her see the world differently. It did the same for me. Instead of looking at the companies I worked for as organizational charts detailing departments and titles, I looked for the opportunities we hadn't yet uncovered.

While I explored the company, its departments, and its people, it would have been easy for me to play it safe and ask the standard get-to-know-you questions. Instead I approached each interaction like a scientific experiment. I'd start with a question: How do you use your energy to make an impact here? With a little prompting I'd get a glimpse into their work. Next I'd ask participants what parts of themselves they were maximizing in this role and which were more dormant. Knowing that this was an entirely new type of question for most, I stayed patient; often the person turned shy, fearing that they'd appear boastful.

And it wasn't just curiosity about others—it was curiosity about myself. I let myself wonder out loud about things. I gave myself permission to think differently about what a job even meant for me as a person. This curiosity led to increased creativity in my approach to challenges, stronger relationships, and more impactful work.

By far my favorite question to get others' thoughts on was: What should we be doing better or differently to get different results as a company? Sometimes I'd hear about the plastic silverware in the lunchroom, other times about a brilliant idea that would impact our people, our bottom line, or both. With just a little prodding, these individuals who had likely been playing it safe, were empowered to step into a new sense of self.

Learning to lead from where you are

You don't have to leave your job, or even your company, to operate like an intrapreneur.

Snuggle on up next to yourself and get excited about how you might be able to maximize your impact starting right where you are. This is an opportunity not just to increase your reach, but your knowledge of all you have to offer.

Give yourself permission to think and talk differently about your impact.

This will not only inspire fresh ideas from you, but from those you spend the most time with.

Anna Oakes

~

Anna Oakes is a change-maker who helps companies increase workforce productivity and potential so that they can scale with intention and increase company value. Raised by hippies to believe that she can change the world without a cape, Anna combines over seventeen years of experience in the people and culture space with her MBA and real-world experience with small to large companies. She lives outside of Milwaukee, Wisconsin with her husband, Scott, and their twins Asher and Juniper.

---

1. Flaum, J. P. "When it comes to business leadership, nice guys finish first." *Talent Management Online* (2009).
2. Goleman, Daniel. *Emotional intelligence*. Penguin Random House, 2012.
3. *Korn Ferry*. "The link between self-awareness and company financial performance." (2015). https://www.kornferry.com/about-us/press/korn-ferry-institute-study-shows-link-between-self-awareness-and-company-financial-performance
4. Gallup. CliftonStrengths. (2024). https://www.gallup.com/cliftonstrengths/en/home.aspx

EIGHT

Your Reality is What the Other Person Thinks You Said

Nicole Elias Seawell

His first word was "Mama" but when he said that, he reached for his dad.

That might've been foreshadowing where his comfort existed. Dad was his calm, safe place, not me. This was a gut-punch to a loving mother and equally to my pre-conceived notion of motherhood. After a lifetime of meeting and exceeding all expectations, suddenly I wasn't sure if I could be the mom each of my boys desired. How could my boundless, unconditional love not be what he needed? I tried the very best way I knew how, and let's just accept I was beyond competent. People in my life have always referred to me as a "Steel Magnolia"—my sunny, energetic, kindness coupled with a steely strength. That is when it struck me: I needed more ways to do the how. My best, as it was, was not what he needed.

I had three boys in just under four years. Son two had arrived exactly twenty-four months after son one and son three twenty-two months after that. Often I could be found with the youngest in the Baby Bjorn, the toddler sitting on my hip, and the oldest holding my hand. I had seemingly unlimited energy and definitively unlimited love for those blonde-haired blue-eyed busy little boys. I embraced motherhood just like everything to date in my life—to be excellent at it and succeed in it. I was going to be the *best* mom. It was easy and hard in the ways of a typical entry into motherhood with our own special sauce.

I just assumed I had the recipe for a happy family.

The early years sped by in a happy blur. My superpowers of organization and problem-solving were on full display, finding solutions to support my boys to thrive by maximizing the days with enriching visits to the zoo, children's museum, library, park, music classes. My husband taught them to cook and I taught them how to bake. They learned to ski not long after walking and spent many days and nights exploring the beauty of the Colorado mountains. It sounds idyllic. And in many ways it was a beautiful, messy, loud, organized, and sometimes smelly chaos.

Our family hummed along quite well until middle school when the cracks in my mother-son relationships started to emerge. While it is normal that middle school is tough I was rocked by learning that my mothering skills were falling short. What worked for one son did not necessarily work for the other and that perplexed me. What was I missing? How was this not working? Mothering a child like me is easy: mindless habits rather than conscious choices. I have one mini-me kid so for him it was second-hand. But I started to understand that I had more similarities in my natural "operating system" to one boy than the others. How I viewed and interacted in the world did not align as well with how my other boys did. And that lack of alignment sometimes caused disconnection.

I would say something to one son that I thought was helpful and in response I would get looks of utter annoyance, frustration, despair, or maybe a combination of all of these. Sometimes he would just say "yes" to simply make me stop talking. So I would double down, push harder, and try to explain myself more. I did not change tack, I did not back down. I was determined to push for the outcome I believed would serve each of them. I did not *yet* see the issue or that the onus would be with me to find a better way to connect with each son. My way was lauded in the professional world and it was working generally very well with the other two. Could he get on board? The answer was actually no, he could not. *But why not?* It made no sense to me.

There were many small moments in their younger years where they gave me signals that we were not connecting. But they were young and it was not all that complicated most of the time so the lack of connection was not catastrophic. Middle school and into high school allowed those small cracks to become chasms of miscommunication.

COVID-19 pushed us over the edge, exposing all that was not working. I could claim the same generic reasons why my kids flailed and failed during those remote and confused months. But it became clearer to me that my style and the way I would have shown up for online school at their ages—ready, participatory, and excelling—was not each of their ways. I am driven to succeed and progress in whatever I do as a student, a professional, a community member, a wife, a mother. For my sons, especially one, working hard "just because" held absolutely no motivation for my son. The more I said, "You should do *this*," and, "Don't you care?" I was missing the fact that he did not inherently care and especially not under those circumstances.

The result was that the more I pushed, the divide between my son and I grew and grew. We were now completely on opposite sides of our COVID chasm. Did I not understand that he needed social interaction to pay attention? His learning style needed live interaction, not a talking screen. To stay on track he needed more structure to his day as he is creative by nature and will not impose self-structure.

I tried to appeal to their sense of COVID being a shared challenge for us all. I was not seeing friends or extended family or clients either. My extroverted self was isolated too. Instead of my normal social self, I was with three teenage boys and my husband *all* the time. And the golden retriever—thank goodness for the golden retriever. To make the point, I shared with them that their dad and I were making the best of it. Two shook their heads and moved on. But one son looked right at me and replied, "You and Dad chose each other, I did not choose either of you."

Ooooof.

I was at a loss for a while. However, I did not give up. I cajoled. I made bargains by offering rewards and external motivations—but as the semester neared its end things looked bleak. His dad and I stepped up and helped him to learn the materials so he could put these classes behind him. And he did. So now what? We had another atypical year ahead. How would he thrive in college? I am sure he thought getting away from us would be a relief—escaping all the parental pressure and expectations.

THE BIGGEST LESSON I needed to learn was communicating with my children in a way that made sense to them. That was what felt like love to them.

In my search for help, answers, and guidance I was introduced to the Enneagram. The Enneagram delves deep into motivations, fears, desires, and core personality traits. It doesn't just categorize behaviors, it explores the underlying reasons behind them. This dive into understanding my core motivations was quick to apply and provided so much depth to my understanding of self and others in communication, interactions, and relationships. It provides understanding of what was happening under the surface. As an Enneagram Three, I am motivated (not surprisingly) by the need to be productive, to achieve success, and to avoid failure which shows up as hardworking, goal-oriented, organized, and decisive. Skilled Threes are playful, pleasing, giving, and responsible.

From the new understanding and vocabulary around my motivations and that of others, I was able to help my family identify themselves. With that identification I became aware of why with one son my fast, direct, problem-solving orientation aligned so well. He was also fast, direct, action oriented and positive. With the other two I learned a lot about how I could pivot my communication style to their needs in order to have more effective connection.

My a-ha moment was understanding that the effectiveness of an interaction lives with the listener or receiver's ear and not the intent of the speaker. While all of my intentions were loving, my intensity, confidence, and action orientation felt like too much at times.

Over the last several years, our relationships as a family have grown as we use this awareness to connect better with one another. That was part of the magic when I tweaked my approach—slow down, one topic at a time, listening and not questioning, allowing space for processing, agreeing to deadlines not setting them. They would tweak their approach back and we could find a productive middle ground.

Just the other day one of our sons called from college. He had just visited Yosemite National Park and was sharing his experience and awe at its natural majesty. He was telling me about the beauty, his photographs, and the extraordinary hike. When we hung up, my husband asked if he was calling me back, because this son did not typically call just to chat and check in with me. But indeed, that was all he wanted to do. My heart swelled with love and happiness to have my son, unprompted, reach out for me to share a meaningful moment.

It took me years to figure out that the disconnect was our different communication styles, not a lack of love. My love for all my boys knew no bounds but my ability to communicate and connect from early on felt more challenged at moments with two of my sons more than the other. That challenge had the corresponding impact of making the relationship harder and more distant, the opposite of my love for them. I learned to communicate and act as they needed in certain moments, not necessarily what I would have needed at their ages.

THERE IS no magic bullet of communication whether mom to kids, leaders to teams, or teachers to students. We all tend to follow habitual, non-conscious patterns of thinking, feeling, and behavior and this limits our ability to learn new skills and to grow.

If we want change and growth, we must first be aware of our internal narratives that stall our change and then be willing to write new ones. Every person's communication style is also their leadership style. How we communicate is the reality that we create. The recipe for my family was understanding my impact on my boys and learning from there. First, I needed the awareness before I could pivot, tweak, or nudge myself to their needs. Once I had the awareness of my own style, its impact on each of my boys, and the listener's potential communication needs, I moved to building an authentic connection. Lastly, with real connection, I could engage with those beautiful boys for wherever life took us. Enneagram helped us to see ourselves and therefore grow from our natural patterns.

These realizations are not unique to families or the leader being Mom or Dad. The key ingredients of Awareness, Connection, and Engagement (ACE) apply in all relationships and communications, business or personal. If you want better, here is my recipe for how you can do better and create your own secret sauce:

Awareness

- Build your awareness by naming your communication style. Ask yourself questions about pace, the need for detail, conflict style, risk relationship, and decision making style.
- Observe your communication impact on others.
- Observe the way your listener communicates and see where you connect or differ. How is their pace, detail, conflict style, risk relationships, and decision making style? Where do you align or conflict? This identifies opportunities.

Connection

- Use your new awareness to meet the receiver's needs, not just your own.
- Treat it as an exploration and try different approaches. If you are fast, press the pause button on yourself and leave more space for others.

- And try to make a genuine connection. When we connect, we extend grace and patience to others.

Engagement

- With awareness and a connection, a bridge has been built for fruitful engagement. It is futile to try to engage your audience if the other two do not exist.
- Engaging communication yields more satisfaction and better results and creates positive expectations for future interactions.

I LOVE my sons more than anything. Failing to connect with them at any moment held such sadness and mystery for many years. I once pictured myself as Julie Andrews in *The Sound of Music*—I am tone deaf, so it was a stretch—being aware and meeting with each child's needs creatively, energetically, with fun. When it turned out that *raindrops on roses and whiskers on kittens* did not help my mothering, I was temporarily despondent. Yet, I did not need, or choose, to stay in the dark.

Today I enjoy strong relationships with each of them through the fruits of effective communication, and continuously choosing to be thoughtful and individualized in my engagement with each son. I encourage you to step into improved leadership by understanding the impact of your communications then choosing how to do it better. It starts with you.

Nicole Elias Seawell

~

NICOLE ELIAS SEAWELL is an action-based diplomatic bridge-building executive coach for leaders and their teams, an Enneagram expert, and a curious culture consultant. She has a JD from the University of Pennsylvania and BS from Cornell University and has worked with leaders and their teams to leverage their interactions, create inclusive cultures, and optimize outcomes. Representative clients include Liberty Media, Guild Education, McKinsey & Company, ThirdLove, Monigle, Partake Foods, and TripAdvisor. Nicole lives in Colorado with her husband, sons, and golden retrievers.

NINE

Finding My Early Warning Signal

Christine Wenger

I ignored all the small signs along the way. Like how I would pick up my laptop after putting my girls to bed at night, every night and every weekend. I was texting clients while I was "talking" to the person I was with. I would show up at school activities while constantly checking email or thinking about the next place I needed be. My head was rarely where my feet were. I kept doing all the things that working mothers have to do through tears of frustration: take care of a family, be amazing at work, volunteer in the classroom, encourage and facilitate afterschool activities, put dinner on the table, host parties, and keep everyone happy at home. The story I told myself was that I was strong and capable. I could do this. All while ignoring the constant pain in the lower left side of my back.

I kept going.

I would often hear that I have a high capacity to get things done. "We need you to finish that project, but we need you to rescue this off-the-rails client even more!" I remember standing taller immediately after anyone would ask me for help. I didn't want to let anyone down. It felt good to be wanted and helpful.

Many days I felt vibrant, alert, and confident after delivering a project at work, picking up my daughters on time from daycare, feeding them a delicious healthy meal and responding to emails late at night to keep the team moving forward. I sailed my way through those days. Other days my head swirled, was foggy, and felt extremely full. Emails felt like they were coming at me from all directions, customers were finding mistakes, three new issues would pop up for each issue I resolved, and my sleep was minimal; I felt like a fire fighter.

On those days, I began to picture a circus clown with a smile painted on my face, standing on one leg on top of a ball while trying to juggle seventeen spinning gold plates and not dropping a single one. Outwardly I put on a smile, was available for everyone and usually appeared as if I had it all together. Inwardly I moved between confidence, feeling overwhelmed and insufficient. Sometimes I didn't know I was struggling. "This is life, this is how you do it," I thought. "High stress comes with the territory."

I looked around and saw that many other working mothers were operating the same way. Why would I be different? I was holding on tight to having it all. I kept powering through harder and holding on tighter. I'd get a reprieve and smile and say yes to more work and helping others. But the excruciating pain in my back continued to come in twists and turns, like an unrelenting roller coaster. I couldn't seem to get off the highs and lows of the track.

One day I was sharing my frustration with my physical therapist. I had endured five years of doctors' appointments, physical therapy, and debilitating pain since a trip to the ER because I couldn't even stand up straight. She said she'd been trying to tell me, for years, that my brain was playing tricks on me. She pointed me to a class at UCLA on how our brains manage pain.

There I learned that in the lead up that triggered the ER visit, the wires in my brain got crossed and I needed to learn how to rewire them. I had been calling my ability "to get a lot of things done" in life a skill, but it was far from it. My inner dialogue was not in alignment with what my body was trying to tell me. I had mastered plowing over myself and excelled at a high stress level. In fact many people didn't even see the effects I was experiencing. I was locked into my high-stress habits.

Much like when you initially slide down a hill of freshly fallen snow, it can be choppy at first. When you go down the same path again and again, it becomes smoother even faster. Well, that's how our brains work too: it's called neuroplasticity. I had trained my brain to recreate the pain the minute I felt a small discomfort in my lower left back. The path my brain had held onto was the smooth, fast path to stress.

I didn't want to admit that I wasn't managing everything well; my desire to help others got in the way. I was missing a big piece of the puzzle, my awareness of what was happening *plus* the ability to build resilience to bounce back. I rarely paused to check in with myself for if I had, I would have had to admit that I wasn't able to juggle as many plates at once or to ask for help.

I read, listened to podcasts, experimented with various apps on my phone—determined to find what would solve this vicious cycle. I discovered there is healthy stress that moves our lives forward such as new jobs, sending kids off to college, or taking tennis lessons. This stress fuels our growth. Healthy stress is positive. Then there is unhealthy stress, the kind we hear in mainstream media. Not all stress is created equal. I became desperate for a change. It took me a long time to see differently.

OVER TIME I developed and learned to tune my personal early warning system for when I was holding unhealthy stress. I began to see when and how to get off the stress ledge. I became aware of the tap-tap of my lower left back—my loudest early warning signal. I noticed when my shoulders were at my ears, when I would hold my breath throughout the day, when I was short with others, when I wasn't sleeping. Before, I rationalized all of it by telling myself I was helping others and getting lots of things done.

There wasn't one easy solution and I had lots of stops and starts. By far the biggest impact to rewiring my thought patterns and diminishing the pain was learning and experimenting with mindfulness practices. The most impactful was starting my day with a short reset: a mindfulness breathing practice for one to five minutes on most days. I had no idea something that small would be so magical but it is the single most effective way that I have uncovered. It's my morning bliss. If I have a critical meeting or deadline I double my usual time spent in practice.

I learned to recognize signs in my body. Neuroscientists say it takes ninety seconds for you to feel emotion before it moves through your body. If longer than ninety seconds, then you are telling yourself a story that may not be true.[1] By building this noticing (awareness) muscle, you can begin to identify earlier what is causing the stress overload and use the pause to decide how you want to respond.

To retrain my brain and build new pathways, when I felt the pain in my back I started using verbal cues. When people would ask about my back, I would respond in the positive, "I feel good." I also use silent verbal cues. To be a better listener, to give me a moment of pause, I will say a silent "Hmm" as someone is talking. There's an act of hearing it in my head that helps me to sit back, to pause even for a moment, to get curious. Try it for yourself right now and notice what it feels like in your body.

For me there is a slight settling or stepping back that happens. It opens the door for me to invite others to tell me more. It gives me a chance to slow down my immediate reaction and to decide if I want to respond, let it go, or ask a question. Over time, I could feel my body let the tension go.

I have moments where I get close to the stress ledge before falling. The difference is I don't fall as far anymore and often I can pull back before I get to the ledge. That's resilience, my ability to stretch, pull back, and not break.

REGARDLESS OF ROLE or level within a company or family, we all have a stress ledge. Everyone has a story with a stressful event: from juggling too many plates, losing a family member or pet, experiencing their parents health deteriorating, worrying about losing a job, caregiving, the end of a relationship or child life events. When unaware of how stress affects you, it's difficult to mitigate and to see how you may be affecting yourself and others.

What I realized is that while it might have appeared that I was doing well in the eyes of others, on the inside I had many cracks. I ignored the physical signs. I was trying to survive. I put on a tough exterior to fill those cracks. This has changed how I work in teams. I now watch the people I am working with differently, especially those who tend to juggle many plates. I ask them about life inside and outside of work, and really listen. What cracks aren't visible to them (yet)? How are they stepping away to rejuvenate? How can they build their resilience to recover from setbacks and challenges? What can I do to support them through a challenging time? Adjusting work, partnering with others on the team, providing flexibility and even encouraging a different perspective?

We can all benefit from learning to identify our cracks and build our own toolkit. This is what I learned through my years of experimenting:

1. To survive, we often rationalize our choices.
2. Our bodies hold on to stress and we need ways to get it out.
3. We can build the skills to rewire our thought-patterns and our actions.
4. Small consistent practices on most days, works.
5. The *how* (practices) can look different for everyone depending on the day. Some of my favorites include meditation, bike riding, strength training, reading, cooking, journaling, listening to music, travel, going for a walk, or enjoying a cup of tea/coffee by myself or with a friend.
6. People cannot do everything on their own. Boundaries are important, but organizations need to examine how they contribute.

Number six is important. It's not only at home, but also at work, within the groups we belong to and the activities we participate in. With so much change and transformation happening inside organizations, with asking employees or volunteers to do more with less, each of us is asked to carry bigger plates. Although I used to think I could separate home and work, this is not practical. My whole body shows up. I cannot leave part of me at home. By recognizing our own unhealthy stress patterns we can learn to manage ourselves and to recognize and reduce their impact on others.

Being aware of what's happening in my body is my early warning signal. It's a superpower. Noticing when I am tight, uneasy, or in pain, when the stress has built up, when I am at the ledge. My mindfulness brain-training has given me choice over the actions, responses, and thoughts. The earlier you can uncover your early warning signal the more time you have to tune it to move from surviving to thriving. What is your early warning signal? I invite you to notice what's happening in your body, what thoughts arise for you, and to listen to your inner voice. Get curious.

Before my grandmother died, two weeks after her hundredth birthday, I asked for two of her beautiful serving bowls. My hope is that by holding up these bowls rather than plates, less will fall out and my energy and love for those around me will be more stable and resilient. That I might offer a bowl to others to take breaks from juggling. That I cherish my bowls. I am not cut out for the circus. I now know that I need to choose my bowls wisely.

How can you hone your own early signal? If you hold a flashlight to an area of your life, what do you find? Finish these sentences and answer these questions:

- The plates I am juggling are…
- The story my plates are telling me today are… What is an alternate story?
- The cracks I am noticing today are…
- Where do I notice discomfort in my body? Is this a repeating feeling?
- What would benefit me now?

Finding My Early Warning Signal

Christine Wenger

∽

CHRISTINE WENGER brings more than two decades of experience in partnering with leaders to drive transformation using people-focused practices within Fortune 100 companies. Early on as a young working parent, she was locked into high-stress habits. She's continuously learning and sharing on topics of how our brains play tricks on us, developing mental fitness habits, work-life balance myths, and conscious leadership. Christine lives in Dallas, Texas.

---

1. Taylor, Jill Bolte. *My Stroke of Insight.* Hachette UK, 2009.

TEN

The Stink of Misalignment

Nell Derick Debevoise

I chose a spring-weight scarf as my second and third 'alarms' rang. First, the unmistakable smell of my colleague's dark-as-mud coffee wafted down the hall. Second, my husband's daily 'good morning' text chimed with the distinctive alert of the international messaging app we used to communicate across the 2,500 miles that separated us.

I arranged the scarf modestly around my shoulders and neck and headed down the flight of stairs that separated our living quarters from my office at the community center I was helping to establish in Nablus, Palestine.

Walking down the stairs I heard the final alarm that signalled the dawning of another workday: spirited banter in Arabic among the teachers as they carried coffee and leftover snacks to their classrooms, preparing to receive our three- and four-year-old students when the first bus arrived.

I settled in at my desk, opened my laptop, arranged my own tea and incredibly fresh and juicy pomegranate seeds with some of the creamiest yogurt I've eaten, and decided whether it was a day to open the window and let in the crisp dry morning air, or if I would regret letting the chill in to our huge stone building with poor insulation and no central heating.

This start to the day was par for the course. Unless we had international visitors (rare), or I was going offsite to meet a partner or prospective donor (monthly at most), this was how I began my days as Executive Director (ED) of Tomorrow's Youth Organization (TYO), a grassroots community organization dedicated to providing mental health support for children, youth, and parents as an antidote to poverty, conflict, and violence.

But on this particular day these formerly mundane sounds, smells, and tastes had soured. The coffee smelled bitter, not earthy. The predictable ding of my husband's text triggered panic and guilt as I realized I hadn't called him back as promised the night before. My colleagues' banter sounded agitated and immediately sent me into a tizzy about what was to be done about the potential withdrawal I had learned of the day before of an important strategic partner.

Even my sweet pomegranate seeds looked rusty on the snowy white yogurt, rather than the ecstatic hot pink that I usually appreciated before taking my first bite.

I stood at the window, stunned at the obvious conclusion. I was done with this job.

Alignment is a Moving Target

OVER THE PREVIOUS three years I had proudly delighted in serving as the Founding Director of a truly needs-based community organization in the West Bank. We were supported primarily by Palestinian-American business leaders with deep personal and professional roots in the U.S. as well as in the city in which we worked. Giving us access to international knowledge, tools, and funding, this foundation allowed us an unusual blend of responsiveness to on-the-ground needs in the community.

Early in life I recognized my purpose as using my own position and privilege to activate resources that would improve people's wellbeing and growth, ultimately propelling them to their full potential. I passed up a full scholarship to a top U.S. business school to accept the role with TYO because of how well the organization's mission, strategy, and design aligned with that purpose. The founder's values also lined up with mine.

As I had hoped, in my three years as ED, I learned an enormous amount about organizational strategy, behavior, and operations, as well as the community we served. I relished this growth as well as colleagues' and partners' appreciation of my willingness to let them drive our work, leveraging my role as an advocate for their vision and needs. I was also thoroughly enjoying the adventure of living in a foreign culture and language.

That said, in the weeks—maybe even months—leading up to this day, I had noticed symptoms that I now recognize as misalignment. I got frustrated more quickly with my colleagues' very reasonable questions. My energy for seeking the resources I knew they needed waned. I was a less effusive champion for them and 'our kids' when I made trips to Jerusalem or back to the United States.

What's more, I couldn't get past missing a third dear friend's wedding. My husband's text echoed unpleasantly in my ear because I had a strong sense that our marriage might be ending. And I had decided the week before that given the time, expense, and emotional cost I wasn't going to my father's funeral, after years of his struggle with brain cancer.

The stink of misalignment

ON THE DAY OF THE 'SOURING', as I remember it, I didn't make much progress on my never-ending to-do list. This accumulation of professional and personal frustrations and failures had reached a volume that I could no longer ignore.

I was playing a part in having a very dramatic and tangible impact on people's lives. From moms we worked with we heard that after participating in our programs their kids had stopped wetting the bed or were no longer having suicidal thoughts. Indeed, our work was deeply aligned with the purpose I discovered early in life: to provide people with opportunities for growth, regardless of their circumstances.

But while the role I had in the organization fit my purpose, it was no longer a match for how, where, and when I pursued that purpose. I was not best equipped to take our community center to the next stage of growth—serving more refugee families and expanding through the region. Further, I was missing huge opportunities that mattered a lot to me in the personal, family and friends, and community spheres of my potential impact.

So I canceled the day's meetings and brushed off my colleague's request to touch base on our summer intern candidates. I mostly sat at my desk and compiled the list of 'not working' and glimmers of 'what could be' that I realized had also been piling up. I followed up on the global Executive MBA program, hesitantly clicked through a few apartment listings in New York, and reached out to a few long-time friends to arrange Skype dates that weekend.

Recognizing you have a problem is the first step

I KNEW I needed to live and work differently in order to pursue my purpose in the whole-self way that I valued. A lot has happened between that day and writing this chapter, but essentially I saw how the vast multiplicity of paths leads to any single outcome. I understood the high stakes of aligning one's gifts, needs, skills, and desires with the most effective and efficient path toward the change to which we want to contribute. And I grasped the power of considering these myriad possibilities holistically, throughout our work *and* lives.

In my work as ED at TYO I was contributing to my purpose of distributing opportunity more equitably. But when I zoomed out beyond my daily context, it was clear that I was not achieving that purpose in that role as potently as I could elsewhere. The focus for the organization's next stage was refining the content and delivery of our programs. My gifts of actualizing big ideas, bringing international resources and know-how, and getting supporters excited, were not as useful in this stage as they had been in our early years. I had reached a ceiling in my job.

Working for a small, community-based not-for-profit didn't leverage the privilege and access I have (as an Ivy League graduate with blue eyes) to engage private sector leaders in building more inclusive and impactful workplaces, thus influencing hundreds or thousands of employees to activate their own purpose. Further, I was removed from the community of conscious leaders and experts that I wanted to be learning from and collaborating with.

Personally I had underinvested in my marriage in its critical early years, and lost that relationship. My closest friends were starting families, my father's death revealed the fleeting nature of life, and my taste for freedom, adventure, and learning was not being sated. Reflecting on these areas of my life—the things that matter most to me and that all ladder up to the impact I want to create—it became easier to understand why I had fallen out of alignment. It hadn't been a mistake to take the role but my circumstances had changed. So had the inputs required toward my purpose.

A tool to identify and remedy misalignment

THROUGH THIS PERSONAL JOURNEY, and through work with hundreds of professionals on their own paths to purpose, I recognized *mutually exclusive, collectively exhaustive* categories in which we can invest in our desired impact. Those categories describe *when* in our lives (Spheres of Impact) we can make these investments (of time, energy, attention, and possibly money) and *where* in the world (Spectrum of Impact) we can allocate our unique resources.

The Spheres of Impact and the Spectrum of Impact comprise my Impact Dashboard. It is a simple, universal, human framework that reflects the experiences, reflection, and analysis of hundreds of leaders across industries, sectors, backgrounds, functions, and ages, on four continents and over more than a decade.

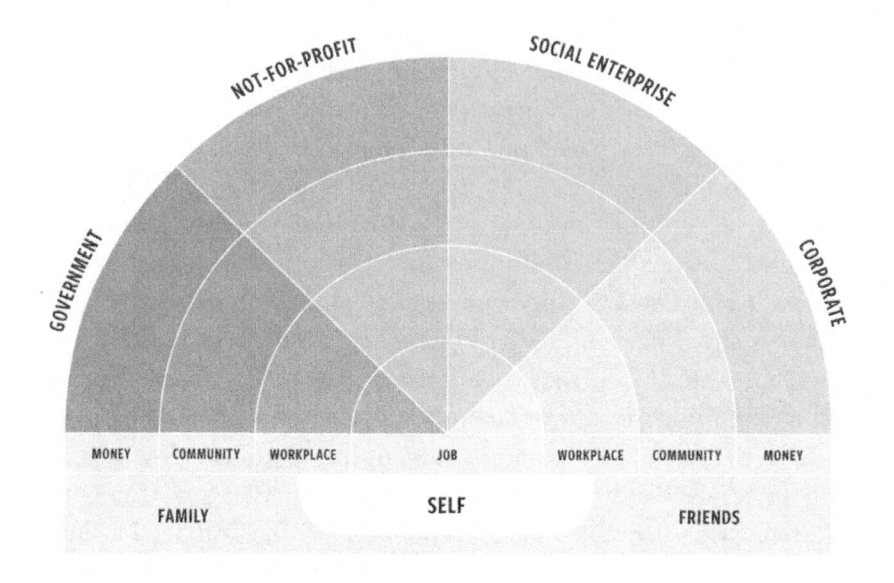

[Diagram: A half-circle dashboard showing sectors around the arc — NOT-FOR-PROFIT, SOCIAL ENTERPRISE, GOVERNMENT, CORPORATE — with labels along the base: MONEY, COMMUNITY, WORKPLACE, JOB, WORKPLACE, COMMUNITY, MONEY, and below: FAMILY, SELF, FRIENDS.]

We—I, along with these clients and partners—have found great value in this structure to map our investments of time, money, energy, and attention in advancing the impact we seek. It provides a snapshot of what we're doing and what we say we are working toward. This information helps us recognize gaps, over-investments, blind spots, and indeed, misalignment. It also creates a baseline so we can make strategic adjustments to our investments in our legacy, and then monitor how they get us closer to the future we're hoping to co-create. Or don't.

The goal is *not* 'doing it all' so that you can rate yourself a 10 out of 10 in all areas of the Dashboard. On the contrary, the idea is to become more aware of where you are already having an impact that you don't give yourself credit for. Or where you might be doing too much, beyond the peak return on those investments and wasting precious time or energy. And then to refine what you do, when and where in your life and the world around you, so that your efforts are optimally aligned with what matters most to you.

The Stink of Misalignment

Individuals who've used the Impact Dashboard in this way gain the benefit of clarity, focus, motivation, and renewable energy for the things that energize them. Further, the Impact Dashboard provides a common language for our teams. When groups of impact-seeking humans share what matters most to them they come to trust each other. This trust enables more satisfying and effective collaboration and ultimately builds efficiency, engagement, and belonging among teams.

Increase your impact by doing less, not more

THE IMPACT DASHBOARD is an action-oriented way to identify our 'one-eight-billionth'—the portion of healing the world that is uniquely ours to do. It's then a way to map and track our investments of time, energy, attention, and money—optimizing the impact they have on our desired outcomes and ultimately, our legacy.

What I say to friends, colleagues, clients, and the public through my writing and speaking is: If you want to achieve the legacy that matters to you, do less, not more.

Get specific about the ways you're investing in each of your Spheres of Impact and where on the Spectrum of Impact you're doing it.

I feel more impactful than I ever have in my current mix of work and life activities. I spend about fifteen hours a week on the Self Sphere investments that I have learned move the needle: meditation, journaling, hard but short weight-training sessions, a twenty-four-hour fast every other week, and horseback riding with a mentor, which links directly to my horse coaching work with clients. While some might scoff at my choice—or ability—to make these investments, I see vividly how they directly and indirectly increase my efficiency and effectiveness in my work. I recognize my privilege to do this, and feel deeply aligned in the way I pay that privilege forward.

My Job Sphere investments are focused on the traditional

corporate sector and extend to public, not-for-profit, and conscious business audiences. I invest most time and energy in refining the content and craft of my message and delivery, as a speaker, facilitator, coach, and author. My Workplaces are mixed. I am a partner in a deeply values-aligned leadership development firm, Faculty for EQUUS—another conscious business—and I'm CEO of a not-for-profit that guides people on purposeful career paths. With these teams I prioritize transparent communication and continuous optimization of our individual energy towards our shared goal of making work healthier, fairer, and more inspiring.

Finally, I make significant Family Sphere investments by pouring into the relationships with my (second) husband and three adult step-children as well as those of my half-sister and mom. Plus of course our two mini Bernedoodles! I am a board member for our statewide association of conscious business leaders and owners, as well as an innovative not-for-profit in New York City. I've made a few values-aligned angel investments, my retirement account is in values-aligned, low-fee funds, and my next Money Sphere priority is to better align the rest of my long-standing equities portfolio. I enjoy great privilege in this blend of investments and am proud of the ways that I pay that privilege forward through these investments toward my purpose.

So, align those investments with your 'one-eight-billionth', doing only the things that only *you* can do uniquely well, passionately, and even effortlessly. And then, with no guilt or shame at the joy and ease you find, take time to revel in the sweet perfume of alignment!

The Stink of Misalignment

Nell Derick Debevoise

~

NELL DERICK DEBEVOISE integrates her studies at Harvard, Columbia, London Business School, and Cambridge with experience on four continents in order to catalyze transformation. She inspires joyful evolution to power the work of our lives, in a healthy, equitable, prosperous, and sustainable way. As a speaker, coach, EQUUS faculty, and internationally best-selling author, Nell integrates neuroscience, behavioral psychology, leadership practice, research, and the ancient wisdom of horses to guide purposeful growth for executives and teams.

Living Authentically

ELEVEN

Unbound

Wilder Horng Brawer

Throughout my childhood a photo hung on the wall of my house, blending into the myriad framed family snapshots. Among pictures of my parents, brother, and various relatives, this one often escaped my notice. It was sepia toned, seemingly from another era, portraying an older woman with her hair tightly pulled back and her gaze stern. It wasn't until I returned to my family's home in Taiwan after my grandfather's passing that I truly saw it again. The framed photo was also hanging in the home where I had been born, where my dad grew up, and where my grandparents had lived until their deaths.

On this particular visit I was struck by the sight of the woman's stoic expression. She sat facing the camera with her feet in positions natural to someone posing for a photo while seated on a stool. But what took my breath away were her feet: tiny, bound feet—each foot would have fit into my adult-sized palm—a stark symbol of her life's restrictions. Despite a seventy-year gap between our births we had coexisted in the world. While she lived with bound feet I lived halfway across the globe, free from physical restrictions but similarly bound by familial, cultural, and societal expectations.

Two questions emerged.

How could she and I, two women separated by only two generations, yet alive on this planet at the same time, live such different lives?

Or perhaps more importantly, what connects us as humans across time, geography, and culture?

Despite immigrating to the United States from Taiwan at age two, I have retained a deep understanding of my Chinese identity. I witnessed my mother's struggles to raise us in a foreign land, adapting to a new language and culture while contending with teenagers who embraced values divergent from her own. It was disorienting to both her as well as to my brother and me. During our initial years in The States her world shrank to a routine of shuttling between home, my preschool, and the grocery store. Her social life was our immediate family and the Goldsteins who lived next door; she had no hobbies, avoided taking risks, and hid behind a language barrier. All this despite being a pioneering woman in Taiwan—among the first to attend medical school just a few years prior.

More recently I found a photograph of my mother from before we moved to the United States.. She exuded confidence and joy, a stark contrast to the fearful, rigid, and risk-averse demeanor she exhibited while raising me. Messages like, "Art is a waste of time," "You need to finish your chores, piano and violin practice," and "Study Chinese before you can play," defined my upbringing and fostered discipline at the cost of joy. I was rarely encouraged to embrace my potential or celebrate my uniqueness. The phrase, "You are a piece of coal, and my job is to chip away a little at a time until you become a diamond underneath," haunted me through college, through marriage, and through raising my own kids. I was never validated as a diamond; it was only the process of being molded to her vision that I experienced. I was admonished to follow rules, not embarrass the family, suppress my interests, obey elders and authority, and to not speak up.

Yet inside I know that continuing to do only as I was told would erode the sense of vitality and aliveness with which I knew I wanted to live my life. There was a *me* inside that wanted to be expressed and my growing awareness of that soon began its emergence.

Motherhood jump-started my journey of unbinding. I began to overtly confront the internalized constraints inherited from my upbringing. I wanted to feel resonance inside and to use this clean and clear energy to guide me. Instead, physical manifestations of anxiety—deep, tight knots in my belly, consistently shallow breathing, constant vigilance—compounded the emotional toll of navigating relationships, particularly with those closest to me.

In group settings I worried that I did not belong and this feeling affected my behavior with peers and the quality of presence I would bring. On the inside I noticed the sensation of feet tightly bound like my great-grandmother's. It happened whenever I felt shame or judgment from others for not aligning with how they wanted to see me, or when I felt imposter syndrome after internalizing the message that I was never enough.

Over time I realized that suppressing who I was and what I wanted for myself created anger that bordered on rage, so much so that when my oldest was born I began seeing a therapist to right-size my relationship to anger. I decided to learn how to control my anger and began looking for tools. I did not want to pass this on for yet another generation to suffer through. I wanted my children to grow up unbound. There was tension between my mother's limited worldview, my rule-bound cultural heritage, and invisible-yet-felt societal systems—tension which catalyzed my journey towards greater awareness and self-actualization.

The path forward

THE JOURNEY BEGAN WITH THERAPY, followed by various modalities like EMDR, sound healing, self-designed-and-led vision quests, meditation, tantra study, plant medicine, energetics, somatic movement, and more.

It was somatic movement, which I discovered early on, that laid a solid foundation for my liberation from things that were not related to my most real self. *Somatic* refers to the body as opposed to the mind, soul, or psyche. Understanding somatic therapy involves recognizing that our bodies reflect how we experience life. It is how we process, metabolize, and store emotions. For example, these stored emotions may remind us of past pain or sorrow and attempt to keep us safe by helping us avoid similar circumstances and perceived danger. Similarly, positive emotions may also be stored in the body and recalled to reconnect us to awe, joy, wonder, and other emotions that boost our resilience. However, when we are unaware of our internal somatic mechanisms we can become trapped in a cycle where we feel less, respond more slowly, or react habitually rather than intentionally. We may stop acting in ways that support our deepest needs, becoming stuck in mindsets, habits, and behaviors that hinder our true greatest good.

At the Strozzi Institute in Petaluma, California, I learned to feel dignity, belonging, and safety in my own body so that I had a body-based home to return to for nurturing, love, reparenting, and sensing. I used these skills to deepen my self-knowledge, self-awareness, and self-trust, so much so that I was able to emerge into a life centered around self-determination. Once numb to feelings and confused by thoughts, I now confidently rely on my body's signals to guide me on the right path. With a growth mindset, it is finally my turn.

It was with the desire to develop a new shape—one in which I could literally stand taller with more dignity in the face of emotional turmoil and suppression—that I dove into somatic work. I learned to feel support at my back and feel forward where I could work with my emotions in real time, including grief. I learned to be more present for my kids. I discovered how to widen my ribs so that I could have greater capacity for connection. I practiced being grounded while simultaneously connecting to expansive source or creative energy. Through body-based activities like mindfulness, aikido, and speech acts (requests, declarations, assessments, commitments), I learned to identify and release patterns that blocked growth. This allowed me to become more resilient, to articulate my yearnings, increase my emotional range, generate a sense of purpose, make intentional choices, cultivate presence, to connect authentically by upholding healthy boundaries, and to respond to pressure with steadfast embodiment rather than distress.

The most important benefits of becoming more embodied are my ever-diminishing need for external validation and the ability to process emotions in real-time. Both allow me to silence the inner critic and stay present and emotionally regulated. I'm able to learn, take on new information, and connect deeply with those I care about and work with. Unfortunately the Western world has relied heavily on cognitive processing, only recently becoming more curious about and exploring the power of our whole-bodied selves.

Somatic awareness

TO LIVE A PRESENT, embodied life that is regulated, purposeful, and authentic, I applied the following somatic arc of transformation.

I learned to observe the flow of my breath and identify where it gets stuck. I used my breath as a signal for getting curious about whatever might be going on inside my body in response to my lived experience at any given time. Because it's easy for us to assign stories to what we feel, I learned to follow my curiosity and explore my felt sensations: temperature, texture, rhythm, flow, and other body-based information that reveal my inner emotional state. It required me to slow down, to feel, name, and breathe—which cultivated a richer level of non-judgmental awareness of myself.

Commitment. Transformation takes time and requires a commitment that you can embody. I use the phrase, "I am a commitment to..." to reinforce my body's acceptance of my desired goal: to soar. For several years I reminded myself that I was a "commitment to soaring" because I wanted to experience stability, calm, and ease as I navigated turbulent years of parenting teens, going through a divorce, financial stress, changing jobs, and moving households. This intentional statement of commitment kept me focused until I was able to embody the sensation of soaring in my life on my own.

Somatic experiencing. Experiential learning is a deep way to make learning sticky. By taking on body-based experiments to access deeper wisdom, I learned to become physically more comfortable with discomfort, to process grief and expand my range to also include joy. Most importantly I learned to self-regulate my emotions in real time when I was triggered. Practices like "Grab, Center, Face" allow your nervous system to experience mild to mid-range triggers in a controlled manner. Instead of reacting instinctively your body practices how to process any and all sensations, get grounded, then face the challenge with a new perspective. Doing this reflexively allows me to stay present in the face of challenge and minimize unnecessary conflict.

Somatic openings. As I became more attuned to my emotions and bodily sensations I was able to create conditions for release. Somatic bodywork, involving specific holds by a skilled practitioner, helps relax the nervous system and release tension or trauma. Somatic practices can also do the same. A co-regulation session with a somatic coach can help you feel emotions that have been shut out over time. Releases that may look like shaking, vocalization, crying, or more intense physical responses, can move the pent-up energy through your body, helping you shift into a new way of being that has greater capacity for feeling, connecting, and authenticity.

REFLECTING on the journey from my great-grandmother's bound feet to my own quest for freedom, I see a profound connection between our lives despite the vast differences in our circumstances.

Her bound feet were a visible manifestation of societal constraints. My bindings were invisible but equally restrictive.

The journey of unbinding is not merely a personal endeavor but a universal human quest.

Each of us has the opportunity to live a fulfilling life and the quicker we learn to unbind ourselves from what impedes our growth, the more we can access the wholeness of ourselves. By embracing self-discovery and, specifically, somatic practices, I learned to unbind myself from these constraints, allowing me to live a life that is more joyful, vibrant, full of feeling, and truer to my authentic self.

Through somatic awareness, commitment, experiencing, and openings, I learned to transform my life and, in turn, to create a legacy of freedom for my kids and their future generations, as I honor my great-grandmother's (and mother's) legacy by becoming unbound.

Wilder Horng Brawer

~

WILDER HORNG BRAWER works to bring more aliveness to people, teams, and organizations. Working at the intersection of experience design, master facilitation, rites of passages, and human consciousness, Wilder works with clients that range from educational institutions to biotech, fintech and ag tech startups, to global multinational companies. She is a co-founder and CEO of Intune Collective, a business strategy and human development consultancy based in San Francisco. As a trauma-informed somatic and energy mastery coach, Wilder's life's work is to help people and organizations evolve, flourish, and embody their core purpose.

TWELVE

Opening Doors to Discover Me

Lisa Foulger

Recently, while vacationing in Grenada, Nicaragua, I was awestruck and deeply moved by the many large wooden doors—artistically carved masterpieces—lining most streets as the entrance to homes, businesses and hotels: portals of sorts. Rich for the eyes, the bright colors served as a rainbow as we drove down the narrow streets, taking in the majestic artwork.

Doors are dear to me. They represent an intriguing passageway into the unknown. And while some doors may be better marked than others, we don't own any doors. It is up to us to muster the courage, desire, interest and fortitude to open each door and embark upon the unknown journey.

Many of my life experiences have included sudden unexpected events that, once embraced, have led to incredible insight, learning, and pure joy. I now appreciate that had I tried to orchestrate my way or waited until I knew more, I would have robbed myself of the spontaneous richness that arose and the awe-filled journey that naturally unfolded.

I vividly remember my first solo international adventure at seventeen, leaving for a foreign exchange trip after high school. I had studied the requisite two years of a foreign language in high school and this was an opportunity to test my Spanish and see how far I could get living a month in Southern France with a family that had a daughter my age. I was excited, nervous and fascinated, brushing up on my Spanish and my top ten survival French expressions. I was under the impression that my host family spoke French and Spanish, but after meeting Florence and her parents I realized they only spoke French and minimal English, so I mustered my best while my stomach was turning circles.

I remember thinking that I had no idea what I was in for.

That thought has surfaced quite a lot in my life path, so much so that now if I don't naturally feel it, I seek it out intentionally. I miss the two-punch combo of fear of the unknown followed by a sense of an impending discovery that delights: pow, pow!

Strapped in and ready for a ride, I joined my host family in their car and drove to their sleepy beach side village, Saint-Mitre-les-Remparts in the south of France. I dozed off on the car ride, jet lag setting in. What a treat to wake up to the most tantalizingly wonderful smells coming from the kitchen when I arrived at their home. I easily assimilated into the long and luxurious, not to mention very tasty, dinner that followed. Not a good cook, yet courting a deep love of eating, I was mesmerized by the divine taste of the French cuisine and flowing red wine. I started to recognize that I was the only one speaking Spanish and my ten-word French repertoire had run dry. Pictionary became our primary mode of communication. This inaugural journey of finding creative ways to communicate while in a foreign country with people I've just met bolstered my adaptability, resilience, and emotional intelligence as well as sense of fun.

Little did I know that twenty years later I'd find myself in a similar predicament.

IN 2008, another door I entered boldly was the opening to our family move from California to Costa Rica where I've lived for the last sixteen years.

It was the realization of a dream to raise a family abroad,

extending outside of our comfort zone, and our young family was open and inspired to seek new experiences. I was all in for this adventure! I took a one-year sabbatical and traded my busy corporate executive role at Hewlett-Packard (HP) for exploration, all while raising a family.

While I can't say I had a lot of free time, I did enjoy the freedom of turning off work and fully immersing my time and energy into this new cultural family experience and taking my second swing at deepening my Spanish. We rented a home on a Costa Rican family's coffee farm and set out finding our way, building new friendships, navigating driving in a city with no addresses or street signs, and settling into a new school for our daughters.

I still remember being in the passenger seat, notepad gripped in hand, scribbling notes of landmarks as our neighbor navigated a series of one-way narrow roads with a scattering of potholes as they drove us to the shopping mall forty-five minutes away from our rural home. With no Google Maps we resorted to directions like, "Turn right at the blue two-story house and left at the church center," all while I was thinking it would be a miracle if we were able to find our way on our own next time—even with notes!

Through our kids' school relationships we built beautiful family friendships, got involved in volunteering in impactful community programs, and our family grew rich from the experiences. Not only did I learn about a new culture and navigate my way in a foreign country, once again it opened up many more doors filled with possibilities for my family and me, both personally and professionally.

Behind this door was spaciousness. I had left the corporate world after a twenty-five year run. A self-acclaimed Type A corporate executive at the time, I lived a full schedule: early morning workout, breakfast and school lunches packed, commute to school and drop off my kids, commute to work, and barely find time for bio-breaks during the day before racing home to a kids sporting match or family dinner followed by helping with homework. If I could stay awake I'd catch an episode of *The Good Wife*.

I was completely out of touch with the idea of creating space. In fact my well-trained knee-jerk response to the concept was, "For what purpose?"

I always had a waiting list of items to slip into any free space. So when I jumped off the corporate bandwagon it was hard to ignore my dog-with-a-bone task focus, a deeply ingrained pattern that fueled a successful career. Yet I was tired and wasn't compelled to go, go, go like the Energizer Bunny. Instead I found that the mode I had been operating under for decades was no longer fulfilling me. I discovered these deeply engraved patterns required a hard reboot, a complete rewiring of my mind, body, and soul.

After leaving HP I still woke up at 5a.m., yet I had no desire to review my to-do list. Instead I started a new morning routine: meditation, spiritual reading, gratitude journal and a dog walk. These changes started dipping me deeper below the surface and breeding curiosity about what I wanted to do with this new gift of time and energy. Not having the work routine certainly afforded me an easy array of surface level activities to let go of, which created new space. What did I want to do with this space? I realized then that I had far more to explore and to learn about myself.

This winding trail of self-discovery offered both highs and lows. My emotions seemed to change frequently, from glee to guilt and a variety in between that gripped me—like riding a topsy-turvy roller coaster, strapped in yet not fully ready to ride. The greatest high was the new sense of freedom that I felt deep within, like an eagle soaring over a beautiful canyon, seeing with awe all the beauty my eyes could take in, all the sounds my ears heard, the exhilarating feeling of air whisking by as I soared.

Could this even be true? I found myself watching a movie in which I was the lead character yet I wasn't directing the plot. Surely I was missing something. Suddenly instead of feeling peace I felt confused. Nowhere to be, no deadlines to hit, no schedule to adhere to. I felt like a kid in a candy store: playful, curious, wanting to try so many new things. Over my working years I'd built up a bucket list of people to spend time with, places to travel to, new adventures to experience, books and hobbies to indulge. It was a new language, one I didn't quite understand, yet I was drawn to learn and felt a sense of struggle in not being ready or willing to learn it just yet. My newly minted child-like state allowed me to revel in the simple things. Freedom felt awesome, yet I also felt guilty, almost self-indulgent.

I gave myself the gift of a year to dabble. During this time I broadened my network, connected and held many expansive, explorative discussions with people—from old friends and former colleagues to new introductions. I truly enjoyed this gift, perhaps even more after it had passed than during the year-long process. As a bonus it led me to my next work gig. In reflection, which I now regularly practice and have gotten much better at, I recognized the beauty of allowing natural transitions.

IT WAS through this trail of discovery, prompted by the space and inspiring conversations that took place during that sabbatical year, that I discovered where my passion, purpose, and talents intersected and joined. I attended a Scaling Up event, led by that global coaching organization that serves entrepreneurs and their leadership teams in aggressively growing and scaling their small and medium-sized businesses.

I'd had my fill of the corporate world yet was still motivated to inspire leaders to make an impact. I was drawn to entrepreneurs who were building businesses as they exhibited qualities that I found myself wanting to foster: adventuresome spirit, risk-taking, autonomous decision making, willingness and hunger to try new things. My new coaching provided the ideal environment to do just that. Twice a year I attended a Scaling Up Global Entrepreneurial live Summit that sported thought leaders from many facets of business, all sharing their ideas and experiences with a large group of entrepreneurs from around the globe. It was an electrifying experience—one of connecting, learning, and supporting that richly fed and inspired me.

I found myself returning to a state of curious exploration, much like I had when I was seventeen. My desire to learn new things was growing and through leadership coaching I wanted to expand my impact further. Suddenly I understood that I could experience both the freedom and curiosity of a child while tapping into the wisdom and resources of a recovered corporate executive in order to forge my own trail. I felt as if a lightbulb had illuminated a new path, one I never would have imagined, and which would not have been possible had I not allowed new experiences and connections.

I was awakened to the idea that the combination of wisdom, expertise, and curiosity powerfully equipped me to lead a life by purpose. I didn't have it all figured out but this in turn fueled new energy, new passion, new inspiration—along with a positive mindset shift that allowed me to find the opportunity and gift in each challenging situation I faced or in every client I coached.

I had a new relationship brewing with spaciousness and with how important it was to cultivate new ideas, reflections, clarity. Filling my plate with busyness was no longer the goal. I shifted towards being much more discerning in what I engaged with and focused upon, and in who I wanted to be in order to drive fulfilment and generate impact. This was my catalyst for going deeper with my heart, mind, and soul: Becoming.

Along the way, I welcomed new experiences that expanded my network and helped deepen my journey: role models, books, retreats, new communities. These experiences served as gifts that I gave myself to take refuge, refresh, refuel and stretch my mind, body and spirit—a source of renewal that filled my tank. They also continue to serve as guides and catalysts to me as I gently navigate my life path, always in transition as I become the next version of me.

Deep questions continue to arise: Who do I want to be? How do I want to show up? What impact do I want to impart on all those who cross my path?

Continuing to forge a life journey of opening new doors and entering new spaces is an awe-walk of reveling in the unexpected adventures and rich experiences that continue to provide joy. Taking the risk of continually saying yes has been an unleashing of my inner soul.

Here are three questions that I invite you to explore in a cozy spot, a quiet space—allowing a generous, uninterrupted span of time, with journal in hand, unplugged from the outer world:

1. What are you courageously willing to say yes to without knowing where it will lead?
2. How can you give yourself luxurious spaciousness in your life?
3. What constraining expectations are you willing to let go of?

Lisa Foulger

~

A dynamic leadership coach with thirty-five years of corporate and entrepreneurial learning and success, including twenty-five pioneering years at HP, **Lisa Foulger** is certified in Scaling Up, Positive Intelligence, and is an ICF Professional Certified Coach. Lisa ignites leaders to excel by scaling their leadership, their teams and their businesses. Passionate about cultivating healthy mindsets, generating transformative impact, and advancing global sustainability, she leaves a positive mark on people and the planet. A proud mother of three awe-inspiring daughters, she thrives in vibrant Costa Rica.

THIRTEEN

Living Your Truth

Missy Bright

A lifelong learner and a self-help junkie, I was born and raised in Minnesota, where we eat hot dish (a Midwestern casserole staple), drink pop (also known as soda), and play "Duck, Duck, Gray Duck." Yes, in Minnesota it's a gray duck (or is it grey duck?). Just ask us.

During my life there I watched as snow days of old changed to the annual discussion of when, and for how long, the "polar vortex" would hit each winter. Every year, I would jokingly ask myself, "Why do I live here?" My reply would always be the same: "I was born here."

Then one day I intuitively changed the question to, "Why do I *still* live here?"

I've always wanted to leave the Minnesota winter but when my niece was born in 2003 the pull to stay and watch her grow up was greater than my desire to leave. But in 2019 I traveled to Phoenix, Arizona to tell my guardian angel, recently diagnosed with ALS, what she meant to me. There I found the place I knew I could call home. It just felt right to me, and I could no longer ignore that inner voice and feeling. I knew I could no longer stay. Little did I know that following my intuition would be the key to living my true authentic self and life.

Reflecting on my life, there are certain truths I've known for some time. These are things that I've felt strongly about or that have resonated with me on such a visceral level (like deep down in my cells or soul) that when I haven't lived my life that way, I've dealt with self-induced cognitive dissonance. For some reason or another I didn't listen. Sometimes I was not in the right place (or headspace), sometimes I let others sway my feelings or convince me otherwise. Mostly I was just not being truly honest with, or true to, myself. I wasn't living my life for me.

Klutzy and very awkward at times, I was the kid who spilled their milk across the table. My nickname was Messy Missy. Even today Grace is definitely not my middle name. But I was also the kid who learned to like liver and onions because everyone else said it was gross and Mom wanted someone to eat it with. I ate it rather than speak up and risk hurting her feelings or insulting my mom's cooking. Unless you pushed some very specific buttons (that only my sister knew), I was the kid who just went with the consensus because it was easier and didn't cause a problem or disappoint anyone else. It wasn't until somewhere in my thirties that I finally told my mom I didn't like cherry pie filling. Prior to this confession, and accidentally the year after it, she frequently made cherry cheesecake for my birthday (which of course I ate).

I wasn't raised in a particularly religious household. My siblings and I were confirmed in a Lutheran church and then given the choice and freedom of whatever religion we wanted to pursue (or not) and how often we wanted to go to church (if at all). Though I regularly attended Sunday service growing up I've never felt closer to a higher power than when I'm out in nature. Laying in the grass under a tree in Minnesota, catfishing in Indiana, or hiking here in "The Valley" (a common name for the Phoenix metropolitan area), it doesn't matter. I don't pretend to know what that larger truth is, I just know I feel different about myself, the world, and my place in it when I am out in nature. Therefore, if you ask me now what church I belong to, I will tell you I belong to "the church of the open sky" (and the sky here in Phoenix is amazing). Nature is my church. I don't need to sit in a pew to commune with my beliefs and what better way to appreciate the magnificence of creation and my immateriality in the scheme of time than atop a mountain with a spectacular 360-degree view? That is another one of my truths, something I've always known and still need to listen to more.

From a very young age I always thought I would move to Colorado. I recall saying I wanted to be able to be outside more and my response to, "Colorado has snow," was, "It melts in a few days or weeks, not months like here."

Shortly after I moved to Phoenix, COVID-19 hit, which turned into a lot of long scenic drives and hiking both on and off the beaten path. I don't recall the actual moment I came to know I had found my true home. I just feel a completely different kind of peace here. Back in Minneapolis I would fill my evenings and weekends with social events and activities only to crash and do absolutely nothing for a weekend to replenish. Now it's the opposite. I rarely go out at night or on weekends, yet I no longer feel the need or pull to do so. After a lot of self-reflection about that wholesale change, I realized I was staying busy to avoid my life, not to live it.

Even when I was packing to move to Phoenix I found my "Eye on the Seniors" article from the local newspaper. It highlighted my time in high school and what was next for me and I was quoted as saying, "In 10-15 years I expect to have the white house with two kids and a white picket fence."

I have honestly never wanted, nor saw, that for myself. I read the article with a deep sadness for both the innocence lost and time wasted. Then I shredded it.

At that time in my life I had said what I thought I should say or what others wanted to hear. I said and did the "smart thing" because I was a "smart kid." Yet that was the opposite of smart. I was entirely un-self-aware.

I was living life for everyone other than me.

. . .

WE ALL HAVE times where we know something deep down, viscerally, on an inner-plane level, within our intuition. Yet we've ignored it, squashed or quieted it, talked ourselves out of it, told ourselves it was nonsense.

Years ago I read about the loss of the gravitational pull because some percentage of loss in the Earth's crust. The book also mentioned a company that made magnet mattress pads which (in theory) help your health by replacing some of the Earth's lost magnetism. At an instinctive level I always wanted one. I can't even tell you why, I just wholeheartedly wanted one. But I wasn't living a life in which I felt comfortable either buying one or asking someone else if 'they would mind' etc. Once I moved to Phoenix it wasn't even a question. I wasn't waiting any longer to buy it. I can't specifically notice a difference, but I don't believe it's doing me harm, so the magnet mattress pad stays. Then a year ago when my left hand suddenly would not stop tingling (constantly for days). When I had exhausted all other options I bought a magnet bracelet that I now only take off for the TSA. Lo and behold, the tingling lessened immediately and within twenty-four hours stopped completely. This week, when my right hand started to tingle, I switched wrists and the tingling was gone in less than six hours, literally as I was reading about how magnets don't really hurt or help. I don't care if it's the placebo effect, science, or something we don't yet understand. It works for me and it's one of my truths.

When I originally moved out of my parents' house and started my career I always knew I wanted to buy organic where I could reasonably afford to. Over the years, I've expanded my desire for more natural ingredients into hair, lotions, cosmetics brands, etc. I use essential oils and natural cleaners and remedies. I love rocks, crystals, and manifestation. I struck the word "worry" from my vocabulary, because there is absolutely nothing good that can come from the word or the thoughts and feelings it manifests. These are things that "speak to me" at my most internal level. Red Dye 40 has been my nemesis for my entire adult life. Something always told me I should avoid it at all costs. I didn't know what it was, I just knew to stay away from it. Yet when I didn't listen I paid the price badly (and yes, I do miss red licorice). Over time I just tried to avoid all food dyes. A recent ADHD diagnosis explains why I had this instinctual feeling and should have listened more and a lot sooner.

Throughout my life I've met many people who don't believe what I believe, don't understand, don't care, who want to judge me, or whatever else. I've endured plenty of jabs, comments, and derogatory nicknames—even from family and close friends—because I believe in "hogwash, fluffy stuff, witchcraft, voodoo" (obviously they don't know what the latter two really are). But when I am true to my authentic self, living the life only I want and can live, no shield of armor is necessary. All the negativity washes right over me (like water off the grey duck's back!). I don't take any of these comments, slights, or insults personally, because these are my truths. They will likely not be yours and I won't judge you if they aren't. I'll come to dinner (if you ask me to), eat whatever you feed me, and be thankful for both the food and great company. If you want to know what I believe, use, or buy and why—just ask me. I'll tell you, and you can take that information for what you want, because only you can find and know your truths.

I encourage you not to immediately dismiss your own intuitive ideas as ridiculous, fantasy, or impossible.

Start getting more curious.

Watch for both internal and external clues.

Do you keep coming back to some thing or idea?

Are you noticing a theme in your life again and again?

Is there a sign or a feeling that is begging to be seen or acknowledged?

Only you know the right questions, as they're your questions and no one else's. You'll never know unless you try, and if you won't listen to yourself, how do you expect others to listen to you?

Though I would love to take full credit for my growth and self-awareness, I can't. It took a cruel twist of fate to bring me to where I am today (literally and figuratively). It's true what they say, "We all die famous in a small town."

When a classmate lost her battle with cancer way too young, I reconnected with another of my close high school friends.

Unbeknownst to many, her mother was my saving grace in high school. She was, and still is, my guardian angel. A short time after reconnection I learned that this other friend had been diagnosed with ALS, a terrible death sentence. Bound and determined not to let her leave this earth without letting her know how much she meant to me, I started traveling to Phoenix to visit her on a regular basis. If it weren't for her being here, and the pain and suffering she endured, I'm sure I would be very busy back in Minnesota still living someone else's life.

There is a beauty in hindsight and self-reflection, but they're also a luxury and if we wait too long they may not be things we can all afford. Time is precious and fleeting. I urge you not to wait for fate but to consciously and purposely manifest the life of your dreams—the life you *truly* want to live.

With that I will leave you with this question: "What do you *already know you know is true* but won't admit to yourself?"

Go live your truth.

Living Your Truth

Missy Bright

∼

Missy Bright is a career human resources professional and lifelong learner. She has attained several human resource and related certifications including SPHR, CEBS, and her CPP. When she is not learning, she enjoys helping and caring for animals, hiking, and the Phoenix sunshine.

FOURTEEN

Perfectly Good Enough

Quentin Finney

More than a decade ago, someone I trusted fully, someone who had my best interests in mind, asked me a serious question that stopped me in my tracks.

"What's your relationship with 'good enough'?"

Honestly took my breath away, bringing the kind of dry mouth that finds you when you feel like you should know the answer to the question in front of you but just can't find the words. Coupled with that familiar sinking feeling in the pit of my belly, I felt my face flush as I struggled to respond while the only thought going through my mind was *perfection is the only thing that's good enough*. I had the felt sense that that wasn't really true, but it had become the only answer that felt acceptable.

I had this crazy belief that I had to be perfect at everything I touched, everything I attempted, or I wasn't worthy of anything at all.

Crazy, because this perfectionistic bent really held me back from seeing my own gifts and true value, when in reality perfection is completely unrealistic and unsustainable, no matter how many great successes I racked up, and in the end the only real result was that my own ability to see my personal strengths was substantially lost in the disparaging internal noise. The more I tried to juggle being the best at all things, the more I suffered, and for a time the inner critic driving me also sometimes manifested as an outer critic of everyone around me. What a horrible way of being, how hard to be around I must have been, both at home and at work!

And then things crashed, giving me an opportunity to take a long hard look at myself and how I really wanted to live my one precious life.

The voice of my inner critic didn't really soften. I came to see, however, that that voice was a protector who cared about me and mostly wanted me to be happy and safe, even though we disagreed on what that really meant.

Spending time with myself, deeply exploring my own consciousness, especially feeling into the innate wisdom of my own body, I became aware that my perfectionism was largely due to a perceived sense of lack, a sense that I would finally have value and worth if I won the next award, got the next certification, led the next winning team, achieved the next bigger title, and on and on that list went.

And yet, I also have had the opportunity to contemplate practices like the disciplined Japanese practice of *enso*—one piece of paper, one brush dipped in ink touching the paper a single time drawing a circle. When the brush is lifted, the *enso* is complete, with no touchups allowed. Whatever the result, good enough is revealed in the perfection of that circle, giving a wonderful chance to watch my own judging mind want to make improvements where none are necessary.

The last few months of working on this chapter have been similar: completely full of competing priorities. I have no illusion that my life is any kind of unique. It's a combination of full-time work, half-time single parenting, and also caring for aging parents as a Gen X son in the sandwich generation. The list of ways I'm called to serve continues. Despite my best planning, I've missed writing deadlines, felt creative blocks that magnified those misses, and had to have some serious conversations with my inner critic, my chief protector who also has no fear or shame around pointing out to me all the ways I'm not good enough (or just plain imperfect) and especially all the ways others around me are doing better than I am at this thing called life.

Enter my journey of self-forgiveness, liberating me from the unobtainable drive to be the best of all things to everyone, instead enabling me to let go of the things that really weren't uniquely mine to do in favor of finding my own magic and focusing my energy there.

This is the story I really wanted to tell here. Yet, in the end, the story that came through me while contributing to this book is one of finding peace in the reality of things exactly as they are—perfectly imperfect in every way. My own personal manifestation of *enso* practice, if you will.

WHAT'S possible for us when we allow ourselves the gift of being good enough? What's possible for those we lead when we recognize how our own internal stories and criticisms are translating into expectations that limit people from bringing their own magic to the world, too?

These, my friends, are questions I get to ask myself over and over and over again, a serious exploration of my own sense of value and worth, and a serious opportunity to revisit what motivates someone toward a relentless pursuit of perfection. In my personal experience, what attaching to perfection as the only acceptable outcome really sets up is disappointment, self-judgement, and unhappiness.

Fortunately, there are ways to work with accepting things exactly as they are, and for me there are five of them I'd like to share with you, hoping you also find them valuable in your own life.

First up: don't plan for ideal conditions. Such a trap this one can be, especially for those of us who live and die by our calendars. Ideal conditions are rarely, if ever, the way things flow, even when blocking focus time on the calendar the way I do. (I'm more than certain that I'm not alone in living and dying by what's on my calendar.) Putting dedicated time on my calendar is also a way to relate to procrastination, but even so, blocked time doesn't block the real world from coming into play, which certainly has happened a lot for me lately. As one example, early into a fully-blocked day to focus on writing, my son needed to go to urgent care—absolutely no way to avoid illness, and as a half-time single parent that care falls squarely on me.

These kinds of reality-based interventions are also a good reminder for taking whatever time is available, as it's available, since small moments ultimately string together as progress. Worth paying attention to is how to bring in self-compassion when things go sideways, because even on our best days, even with our best efforts, we can't control for perfection. Yet we can control for how we relate to perfect imperfection in any given moment, which overall is a better use of our time and energy, and it also models healthy behavior for all those around us.

Second is self-care: don't fail to take care of yourself. When I'm not at my best, I feel a magnified pull toward perfectionism on the road to possible burnout, and I struggle mightily to recognize a good-enough outcome. Thus, for me, self-care becomes a powerful antidote to perfectionism, providing me with a much more balanced approach to managing my own expectations of outcome while fostering my own mental, physical and spiritual health.

Prioritizing this can become a bit challenging in a world that doesn't always prize the sacred pause this requires; being of service to others, however, simply isn't otherwise possible. Spending time in nature is super-helpful for me on all three fronts, as is paying special attention to my diet and sleep needs—when I'm well-rested and well fed, I have most everything I need to engage with the wider world and recognize that true perfection has many shapes and sizes, sometimes even those that surprise me in the best of ways.

The third tool I find support from is: don't compare yourself with others. Everyone's journey is unique, including your own. Harshly comparing ourselves to others is inherently unfair and often overlooks our own individual strengths, weaknesses, experiences, and magic. Relating to this in a healthy way also requires a strong relationship with self-compassion, and I've found that when I've looked too hard at other people's significant wins I'm not noticing that I also have my own.

Rather than constantly pressuring myself to be the best at every single thing I attempt (and believe you me, I've spent a lot of my time believing that was the only path to having value in the world), now I tend to put effort into shifting the focus to making sure I'm primarily comparing myself to myself. Am I doing the best I can in *this* moment, based on the resources I have available to me right now? And since that resourcing isn't always the same along the learning journey of life, what can I learn about myself when I feel I could have done better? What can I carry forward for an even better outcome?

Fourth, a tool to support balancing where I place my attention and energy: don't focus on the misses—focus on the wins. Perfectionism often leads me to obsess over the misses and the mistakes, leaving me feeling unworthy and not good enough, but this too is workable through a balanced shift of focus to pay more attention to wins along the way. Sometimes working through the project as a whole feels like running through quicksand, especially when the timeline is long and the incremental tasks are many.

One missed deadline or overlooked detail, no matter how small, can derail energy to keep going, but a fundamental shift is possible by celebrating each small completion as one more step forward. Momentum builds momentum, and in this way I shift from the drain of focusing on the negative to generating the supportive energy I need. This process unlocks the best possible outcome.

And the last of the five tools I use to support myself when I catch myself drifting into perfectionism is: don't fall into the trap of believing that perfect is the only acceptable outcome. Perfection is an unattainable ideal and often becomes a game of whack-a-mole where the definition of perfect can feel like it's constantly changing. Couple that with the reality that one experience that feels perfect can also increase the pressure for the next time.

At one tech company I was part of, we had fifty-seven quarters of consecutive quarter-over-quarter growth, and the pressure to do it again the next quarter was palpable. Such an operating environment of immense pressure fosters the kind of risk avoidance based on fear of not achieving perfect results. Who can thrive in that kind of environment? No task or project will ever be completely flawless, but sometimes pointing at perfection without attaching to it as the only acceptable outcome serves to unlock the possibility for excellence—something truly worthy of celebration.

I'm happy to share these five tools, and I hope you find them as valuable supporting your own journey as I do.

I'd like to leave you with a simple, single question to work with for yourself as you explore your own relationship with and possible attachment to perfectionism—though it comes with an additional requirement for equal parts of grace, self-compassion, and self-forgiveness:

What's *your* relationship with good enough?

Quentin Finney

∽

QUENTIN FINNEY is a human, father, best-selling author, international certified mindfulness teacher, member of the Forbes Coaches Council, and long-time meditation practitioner. After holding operational and executive leadership roles with organizations including Google, Red Hat, EMC, and six startups, he has spent the last decade consulting and coaching, helping others as they discover the inner wisdom they don't always recognize they have—and he firmly believes we're just not meant to do any of this alone.

FIFTEEN

From Inner Critic to Inner Peace

Tricia Livermore

My self-awareness journey feels long and arduous. As I sit here writing I'm reflecting on key life moments that brought me a greater awareness of who I am and, eventually, whom I consciously chose to become.

In my thirties as a post-Catholic, I had a belief that there was something more than just our physical body. I read many books to create my foundational belief based on what resonated with my soul. At the same time I realized my belief system was quite different from most people's so I kept my faith hidden and shared it only with a select few people, for fear of what others might think of me.

When my son was four he came racing from the back of the house and said he didn't want to go alone to the bathroom because Grandpa was back there. My son was aware enough to know Grandpa had died a month earlier; he went to his funeral services. I asked him why he thought Grandpa was back there and he said, "He's sitting in the spare bedroom."

I picked him up and we went to the bathroom together. "He's gone now," my son said.

I had always believed that our soul lives on in a different

dimension and this experience with my son proved it to me. It opened my awareness to sensing loved ones when I perceived that they were nearby.

Reflecting on the educational system and my early career in corporate America, I realized how much I had been conditioned to act like a stereotypical man. What was valued in the world and in business were intelligence over emotions, analytics over intuition, structure over creativity, stoicism over authenticity. I didn't challenge these things because my goal was to climb the traditional corporate ladder for power and prestige. I even completed an entrepreneurial MBA program in order to build a hot-rod shop with my partner, creating the business structures while he created the masterpieces.

Fast-forward to my promotion to director of portfolio management in 2012. Above all, my aspiration was to embody the type of leader I had always longed for—one who prioritized the individual over the tasks at hand. My aim was to forge genuine connections with my team members, to comprehend their motivations and aspirations. I sought to uncover their passions and latent talents and to leverage these to their fullest potential. Additionally I placed significant emphasis on promoting work-life balance as I believed it was crucial to lead by example. Guiding my team members to develop in areas that resonated with their personal goals was also a top priority.

By 2016, as a pilot participant in an executive leadership program, I for the first time in my career had learned how to connect at a deeper level with my peers. This was the first time I learned how to truly build on another person's offer instead of trying to get them to see from my perspective. I went on to teach other teams in the broader tech organization how to utilize this approach in helping tech teams co-create solutions. This fueled me to become the change agent for my organization, creating a three-year organizational strategy to support people in their professional growth and to elevate our tech tools and processes.

In my career I prioritized building meaningful relationships and nurturing personal and professional growth, but my authenticity often attracted backlash and betrayal from others. Despite striving to be the leader I never had, I faced increasing opposition as I leaned into my true self. Seeking support, I enlisted an executive coach who helped me clarify my values and recognize my burnout. But in October 2018 my career took a drastic turn when my role was unexpectedly eliminated during a strategy meeting in front of my peers. I felt betrayed by my leader and isolated by HR. Despite the initial shock and devastation I realized this was an opportunity to break free from a toxic environment. In February 2019, after a fruitful twenty-one-year career, I was laid off, prompting a mix of emotions from heartbreak to relief. While uncertain about my future I recognized the invaluable lesson this was for me to up-level who I was becoming, with the chance for a fresh start in my career.

With the help of my executive coach I could see my inner critic for the first time. I named my egoic voice Lucifer, from the TV series wherein the character by the same name wants to do good but doesn't yet know how.

But in reflecting on everything that had come before, the thing that struck me most was that people and relationships matter perhaps more than anything else. With a greater awareness of the types of relationships I was seeking in my life, I made a conscious choice to end my relationship with my mother. She had made a choice which left me feeling completely unloved and betrayed. This triggered anger, resentment, and depression. I quickly started EMDR and neurofeedback therapy in order to lessen the pain from the event.

My foundational spiritual beliefs are that we choose our parents before coming into this physical body, and that we have a blueprint for the lessons we seek to achieve. Therefore I believe everything happens *for* us instead of *to* us; there is something to be learned in every situation. This philosophy helped me to see this as an opportunity to learn self-love. My mother was seventeen when I was born and there was a lot of shame then around teen pregnancies. I believe this created resentment within her and impacted how she treated me. The guidance of a spiritual counselor allowed me to see my mother's inner child, who had never received the love she needed. This brought me greater peace around her unloving behaviors and eventually I learned to forgive her, knowing I would never receive an apology, and to accept what is.

This catalyst gave me the courage to make some fucking scary life choices.

I'd been married for twenty years and over the last decade we'd grown apart. The more I continued to grow in my awareness the more we drifted apart. Years prior, I made a conscious choice to stay in the marriage because I loved being within a family unit. We sought counseling together and individually, but never found anyone who could help with our core issues. We'd talked about getting a divorce the year before but neither of us made the final decision. Sitting at my desk writing in my journal about how miserable I once again was, I had an epiphany: *I can't do this another day, another month, let alone another year or decade.* The longer I stayed the more I was losing myself.

I asked him to come into the office. "We're done," I told him. "I can't do this any longer. I'd like you to move into the spare bedroom and agree to an amicable divorce without lawyers like we said we were going to do last year."

Since he doesn't like change he became quite emotional. As I sat there listening I felt completely at peace with this long-overdue decision. My next thought was, *Life is going to change dramatically and it will be tough but I will get through it.*

There was no way I was turning back.

Shortly after I left my job amidst a battle with burnout, divorce, and depression, I was diagnosed with the Epstein Barr virus, marking a period of intense physical and emotional turmoil. Physical symptoms had plagued me for years: chronic fatigue, gut issues, food intolerances, mild arthritis, and severe headaches. Their compounding led to what I can only describe as a major dark night of the soul.

Determined to reclaim control, I immersed myself in psychoneuroimmunology and epigenetics, both of which recognize the profound influence of spiritual belief on physical well-being. With a new-found understanding I embarked on a journey of holistic healing, prioritizing self-compassion as my guiding light.

Over the following year I dedicated myself to restoring my physical health—delving into meditation, conscious language, and the intricate link between emotions and energy systems.

A YEAR LATER, I could see the light at the end of the tunnel.

I ventured into solo entrepreneurship as a business coach and mentor, aligning my values of learning, integrity, and spirituality with my mission to reintegrate humanity into the business landscape. This pivotal shift not only solidified my sense of purpose but also provided clarity on my strengths and aspirations. As I continued to evolve I discovered the transformative power of HeartMath in managing emotions and fostering self-awareness. Through this practice I uncovered deeper layers of my psyche, shedding light on my persistent need for external validation and recognition. Armed with this insight I resolved to help others overcome their inner critic and to find peace through emotional regulation—thus charting a path of service and fulfillment in my professional journey.

After the pandemic I was yearning for teamwork and in August 2022 transitioned to a part-time program director role at a local non-profit, on a team of four, executing a leadership development program and organizing a holistic wellness conference for women. Concurrently I pursued formal coaching training and earned a certification in Emotional Intelligence. But a year later, the arrival of an interim CEO triggered panic attacks. Her inability to lead consciously prompted my resignation. This small-scale dark night of the soul moment led me to re-evaluate my life's direction, to delve into spiritual-based literature and to embrace practices of peace and harmony. With renewed focus I resolved to rebuild my coaching business and gave myself a year to establish a sustainable income.

In my ongoing journey toward self-awareness, numerous valuable lessons have shaped my path and outlook on life. These life lessons provided a foundation for understanding how we all operate and the need for greater acceptance and compassion. These lessons also strengthen the five primary aspects of emotional intelligence:

self-perception, self-expression, interpersonal relationships, decision making, and stress management.

Prioritize self-care. Permit yourself to rest more than usual, create a list of self-care activities, and assess and adjust your relationships and environments so that they align with your well-being needs. Some self-regulation practices include automatic writing (journaling), centering practices, meditation, or simply breathing more slowly and deeply.

Cultivate deep relationships. Invest time in building and nurturing supportive relationships to enhance overall well-being. Build community even if it's just a handful of people who feel supportive, because people in community experience increased well-being. Join a life development group that utilizes social therapeutics for emotional workouts with others.

Uncover your truth. Identify and understand why your core values are most important to you, set daily intentions, seek feedback and reflection from trusted sources, and align your decision-making to your deepest truth of who you are. Create consistent daily practices to align with your higher wisdom.

Embrace courage. Courage appears when you confront fears head-on by stepping outside your comfort zone to foster growth and development. Be surrounded by supportive people when making new choices.

Embody self-compassion. Radical self-compassion and an extra dose of grace are required when the overthinking, ruminating, looping inner critic starts to spin out of control. Prioritize compassion as a guiding light in order to ease internal suffering.

Make peace with your inner critic. Our mind is wired on past experiences that are utilized for survival by keeping us in our comfort zone. When we observe the inner critic with active self-awareness we can see the pattern of fear coming to the surface. With courage and compassion we allow the voice of our higher intuitive wisdom to acknowledge the inner critics' concerns and we can move forward together.

Trust the universe. Generate positive thoughts and emotions to raise your consciousness, release attachments to expectations or outcomes, have faith in yourself, and trust in the universe's plan for your journey. Know you are always connected to the divine.

Create a nightly gratitude practice. Reinforce your higher levels of consciousness with gratitude for all that you have.

As I have honed these lessons over many years I've come to appreciate the self-awareness journey itself. Patience, self-compassion, and grace provide me with profound peace in my life. I believe when we each do the inner work to heal, grow, and live in the present moment, we model for others how to be in the world.

For the longest time I wanted to *fix* others, then wanted to *fix* myself—but we don't need fixing. To be who we are meant to be in the world we need care, support, courage, self-awareness, and an intention of growth. Our relationships organically change as we attract new people and others fall away because we've elevated our energetic system to attract something entirely new.

It's not an easy process, but the journey is worth it.

TRICIA LIVERMORE

Tricia Livermore

∽

TRICIA LIVERMORE is the founder and coach of Soul Business Advisor, her mission: to reignite humanity by guiding individuals toward inner peace and harmony through heartfelt connection. With a profound passion for resolving inner conflicts, realigning values, and rejuvenating spirits, Tricia taps into her clients' inner wisdom for profound self-discovery and personal growth. She offers individual coaching and Life Development Group coaching to ease the burden of our inner critic while strengthening emotional intelligence through a supportive community.

Coming Back from the Edge

SIXTEEN

The Unrevealed Masterpiece Within

Teri Swope

"My brother died last night."

These are the words I told my boss over the phone that cold Monday morning. In the wee hours of the previous morning my twenty-one-year-old brother's truck flipped multiple times down the highway and landed upright, without him in it. The coroner said he died instantly. *Instantly.* I had talked to him four hours earlier. How is someone here one moment and then *instantly* gone? How can a human being come into the world only to be taken out of it at the beginning of their adult life? What's the point of life? Of death? Of getting out of bed?

This was my first experience of someone close to me dying and it propelled me into a deep dark well of utter confusion. I had started the prior weekend looking forward to celebrating the birthday of my youngest brother, Dylan. My other brother, Josh, died on Dylan's eighth birthday.

A week later I was back at work. I'd arrived at work an hour early that morning so I could make my way to my office without seeing anyone. I sat alone in my office and stared out the window. The street below was bustling with 'normal' people going off to start their 'normal' workday. There was nothing normal about that morning for me. My office didn't look or feel like the same place I'd left a week before.

I wasn't ready to be at work. I wasn't ready for the stress, the sympathy, the façade. I wasn't ready to act like I cared about the petty, meaningless crap that filled my inbox and calendar. I wasn't ready for the energy it was going to take to act like I was okay.

My boss's assistant knocked and said he would like to see me. *Here we go.* Of all people I wasn't ready to pretend for, he was at the top of the list. I walked into his office, sat down, and fixed my gaze on the obnoxiously large conference phone in the center of the table. We sat in silence. The silence was just the space my barely-contained grief needed to rise to the surface.

"I'm so sorry Teri," he said.

My shaky voice replied with, "I'm fine. Just please don't make me cry."

And with that I abruptly left his office.

I WOULD REALIZE LATER that it wasn't just grief that was welling up in me that morning in my boss's office. It was also shame. Shame for being an emotional wreck when I was supposed to be—had a reputation as—a strong, decisive, emotionally-balanced female leader. When I said, "Please don't make me cry," what I meant was, "Please don't see me for the raw authentic human being that I am."

I didn't want my boss to see that behind the curtain of the good work I did from eight a.m. to five p.m. (or seven, or eight)—there was a raw, vulnerable, hurting young woman. I was almost apologetic for bringing that version of me to work. So I hid her away. I'd allow the wounded version of me to surface outside of work. I sought counseling, cried with my family, and began a spiritual journey that would ultimately lead to some of the answers I so desperately sought. But at work I was buttoned up. Confident. Decisive. Poised in a pencil skirt. Nothing to see here. But also, don't look too closely.

A year or two later a woman on my team lost her sister in a tragic accident. When she came back to work I approached her desk to express my deep and heartfelt condolences. After all, I knew her pain.

"Thank you. I'm fine," she said with dark glasses and tear-stained cheeks, and turned away.

I'd done enough personal reflection and soul-searching by this point to know exactly what I had done to illicit this reaction. I'd modeled the way. I had modeled what it looked like to bring only the shiny parts of myself to work. I had created a workplace where it was not safe to be fully human. My way of leading did that. I did that.

That experience, which took place more than twenty-five years ago, woke me up. It inspired me to pursue a different way of leading, a more human-being way of leading where we honor the wholeness of who we are, not just what we do. It woke me up to a deep love for all people, for all of our pain, starting with my own.

The revealing process

I'D LIKE to say that my leadership changed from that day forward, but alas that's not how transformation works. Most of us have to walk the path, allowing life's experiences to chisel away at the unoriginal parts of us to reveal the masterpiece that has always been there.

The path to unleashing the highest version of our leadership starts with becoming aware. There is no route to higher ground other than through the tunnel of our understanding of who we are, what we value, why we're here, and what we've been taught to believe (or what we think we 'know') about ourselves, about others, and about the world around us.

So how well do you know yourself?

What makes up the unique human that is you?

It's a simple enough question, yes? I know that I like salty food (the salt often added before tasting), travel, fresh flowers, the smell of fresh-cut grass, playing laser tag, all the different ways water makes sound, reading, writing, and yoga. I also know that I don't like perfume (on me or you), snakes, arrogance, the smell of dog pee in the house, or any color or shade of meat. While these attributes illustrate a tiny bit of what makes up my humanhood, it really says nothing about who I am under the top layer of my worldly preferences.

The different and much more important question is: Do you know who the 'you' is beneath all the various descriptions of your humanhood? Not from the perspective of the roles you play in your life, but what makes up the *essence* of what and who is beneath the surface of your thoughts about who you are. Not so easy anymore, huh?

Have you ever looked out over the ocean past the waves toward the horizon? There in the distance the horizon appears to be a flat blue plane of peace, serenity and seeming nothingness. But beneath the surface is a whole complex ecosystem teaming with life and potential. According to the National Oceanic and Atmospheric Administration only about 5% of the world's oceans have been explored. The remaining 95% is still unknown.

Such is the case with our own inner being.

Most of us have hardly scratched the surface in terms of understanding who we really are and what our potential is. And just as the ocean requires study to understand the fullness of what is beneath its surface, so do we. Understanding our potential requires intentional study and reflection, and a sharpened chisel.

What do you believe?

WE WALK through the world thoroughly convinced that the things we believe about ourselves and the world around us are indisputable facts. We also believe that what we know is pretty much all there is to know, especially when it comes to our potential. We take the steady stream of self-deprecating thoughts that flow through our head, usually unchecked, as the gospel truth.

When asked, "Who taught you to believe that?" we reply with, "What do you mean? No one taught me, that's just the way it is!"

And then we scoff and storm off, insulted at the insinuation that we have any power in changing our plight in life: "How dare you!"

The reality is that what we believe is usually some distorted version of the truth or maybe just a flat-out lie. In his book *The Four Agreements*, Don Miguel Ruiz calls this "the liar in our head". The liar in our head is the self-proclaimed spokesperson for what we believe. For example:

Liar: I'm lazy and should be more productive.

Underlying belief: I'm not worthy of rest.

Liar: I'm selfish if I don't give everyone what they ask of me—money, time, attention, love.

Underlying belief: Others' needs are more important than my own. I'm not worthy of making myself my own priority.

Liar: I'm never going to have enough money.

Belief: Money is scarce and supposed to be hard to come by. Only a few have enough to be comfortable. I'm not one of those few.

Liar: My physical body is not attractive. My body should look differently.

Belief: How I look is more important than how I feel. What other people think about how I look is more important than how I feel.

Liar: I'm going to be sick because it's in my genes.

Belief: My body and my wellness are not mine to control.

If any of these sentiments feel vaguely familiar, it's because you're human. Every single one of us is infused with a set of limiting beliefs that creates the script for the liar in our head. The liar's script depends—actually thrives—on our attention to stay alive.

Once we gain enough awareness to recognize thoughts that don't serve us well and that make us feel like we're not enough, we have the power to actively choose whether to believe those thoughts. Lack of self-awareness keeps us in the dark, dragging us behind the wagon of our runaway thoughts. Awareness puts us in the driver seat, where we are in charge of where our thoughts will take us. Doesn't it sound amazingly liberating to know that you can actually be in charge of how you think, feel, and act throughout the day and throughout your life?

Unfortunately few of us take ownership of this power. Few of us recognize that we're being dragged behind the wagon, much less that we have the power to stop it, get up on our feet and unhook ourselves. Conditioned thinking keeps us deeply committed to believing things that just aren't so.

Over the centuries, we've been slowly convinced (conditioned) to shut down the flow of our internal knowing while turning up and subscribing to what the world says is normal and acceptable.

Where we learned that that was a good idea is beyond me.

After all, much of what we accept as normal social behavior or policy is some version of seriously jacked up. For example, it's considered entirely socially normal to consume what are scientifically proven toxic substances (fast food, sugar, alcohol—to name a few). It's broadly accepted that killing people in the name of (fill in the blank) is just and righteous. The inhumane and oftentimes torturous treatment of animals is broadly accepted as a means to mass producing what's for dinner. And yes, I'm going to go there: how ever did we all get on board with the mandate to keep our physical distance from every other human being, even our family members? Yes, that was a government mandate but we all agreed to it and enforced it through social shaming, and we are still suffering its effects. Now, you don't have to agree with me on any of this. In fact, please don't! Our complacent agreeing to stuff that we don't believe is true for us is how we got in this mess to begin with.

My point is: find and follow *your* truth. Uncover the beliefs that aren't serving you and do the work to change it.

I think it's fair to wonder why our human experience begins with the creation of false beliefs, which we then spend a lifetime trying to overcome. Perhaps it is, as Hinduism teaches, that we are here to work out karma, that our souls actually chose this journey and these life experiences to help us settle an unpaid debt.

But why do we need to come into this human incarnation and suffer through unconsciousness? Why can't we sort it all out in the spirit realm, where things are a bit less chaotic?

The Unrevealed Masterpiece Within

Hell if I know! All I know is that there is a way to transcend this lowly, limited, human condition that we've collectively created for ourselves and to ascend to an awareness of the limitless potential within us.

I've seen it. I'm experiencing it. And the fact that you're reading this book means you are too. The masterpiece within you is whispering and the sharpened chisel stands at the ready.

Are you ready?

Teri Swope

∼

TERI SWOPE is the CEO and Founder of SwopeLight Consulting, a leadership training and consulting firm. With three decades of leadership experience, she has witnessed and informed organizational transformation through conscious leadership. Teri believes deeply in the power of storytelling to awaken people to their highest potential. She holds a BBA in international management, multiple leadership certifications, and is a certified HeartMath trainer.

SEVENTEEN

From Pain Management to Pain Free

Alec Kassin

At eighteen I was obsessed with becoming a professional cyclist. While naturally athletic, I was a small and sensitive boy who grew up feeling like he had something to prove and needed to be perfect in order to excel. A head shorter than many of my friends, I was elated to carve out my own athletic niche where my size would be an advantage, not a hindrance.

Despite possessing no special talent, I went from being one of the slowest riders in my freshman year of high school to the highest point-scorer on the California State Champion mountain bike team my senior year. I held a professional mountain bike license at eighteen but after one too many serious injuries I switched to road-racing full time.

My priorities were, in order: cycling, school, everything else. I had three bikes squeezed into my UC Berkeley dorm room and instead of the enticing nightlife that captivated so many college freshmen, I was in bed early on weekends and ready for my four-plus-hour rides—rain or shine. My obsession extended off the bike too: if I wasn't riding I was probably thinking about it. I would even meticulously clean my bike chain with a Q-tip before races. Nothing, and I mean nothing, was to be out of my control.

When my freshman year ended in June 2011, I was ecstatic to pour all of my energy into my dream that summer. I had my work cut out for me: I had progressed quicky from racing against novices to competing against professionals in about two years and I'd soon be entering my biggest race to date, one that Lance Armstrong had won two years prior.

Nine days before that event my life would change forever.

Riding on a bright and sunny Northern California afternoon, I approached a hill that I'd ridden hundreds of times before. I stood up on my pedals, body swaying from side to side. All of a sudden it happened. A crippling pain surged diagonally across my back. It was like a bolt of lightning had struck me. I let out a cry of agony and winced in pain. What had just happened? I hadn't crashed. I hadn't been hit by a car. I was just riding along. *What happened?*

The pain was so intense and my back so stiff that I couldn't bend at the waist. A few days later my chiropractor, in words that would haunt me for years, said, "Don't worry; two weeks and you'll be back on top."

Two weeks quickly turned to five months and I wasn't getting better. I watched that big race pass me by and I realized something was seriously wrong. Pain was impacting my entire life. It roared when I sat, making it difficult to concentrate in my lectures. My social life became limited as a sense of depression slowly engulfed me. Being unable to ride my bike, it felt like both my identity and my dream were being ripped away—and I was powerless to stop it. My cycling team moved on. I watched friendships wither away. I came to the hard truth that the earth was continuing to spin while I was stuck.

I finally got an MRI which confirmed my fears. I was diagnosed with ruptured L4-L5 and herniated L5-S1 spinal discs.

"I'm pretty sure this is what's causing your pain," my doctor said.

While he was optimistic that I would make a recovery, he wasn't sure when. But it was years, not months.

Given the severity of the diagnosis, I received spinal injections and surgery was discussed. I continued to see back specialists, chiropractors, physical therapists, acupuncturists, energy healers. You name it, I probably tried it. And being a detail-oriented perfectionist desperate to heal, I followed their advice to the letter. If I was prescribed exercises, I did them. If I was told to avoid certain activities, I would. Time after time, I'd put my faith into these practitioners, expecting them to fix me, and after a few months I would leave their practice discouraged and depressed.

The dread and overwhelm at the thought of suffering through another semester led me to withdraw from college. This was the lowest point of my journey: at home with my parents, on opioids, spending my days lying in bed, eating my meals standing up. In my childhood bedroom, I had a swinging net chair that hung by a chain from the ceiling. Lying in bed, it was directly in my line of vision. In dark moments I would look up at the chain and see hanging myself on it as my way out. Some days I knew I was being dramatic. Some days I surprised myself that I wasn't.

MY PARENTS KEPT ME GOING. Once, after a particularly deflating medical visit, I was lying in bed when my dad came in. I shared how hopeless I felt. He replied with the exact words I needed to hear: "We'll keep trying until we get it right."

Strangely, I began to notice an odd pattern with my pain. I could have days where I did everything my practitioners said to do —ice, core exercises, avoid sitting—and be in immense pain. But I could have less pain on the days when I did the things they said not to do. Some days, pain would be more severe on my left side than my right. Other days the opposite. If this ruptured disc was causing my pain, why was it producing such varied symptoms? It wasn't until my mom, a librarian, gave me a copy of *Healing Back Pain* by Dr. John Sarno, a Professor of Rehabilitation Medicine at NYU, that I got some answers.[1]

Dr. Sarno pioneered the idea in Western medicine that physical abnormalities—like my ruptured disc—don't always cause pain, and that in fact the brain can be responsible for generating pain as a 'danger signal.' Sometimes that danger signal can be turned on from stuffing down our emotions (especially anger). Other times, it's a conditioned response to physical activity that we've developed over months or years, like Pavlov's dogs salivating at the sound of a bell. Most importantly, Sarno proved through successfully treating tens of thousands of patients that if you're willing to take responsibility for your healing, chronic pain is fully reversible without drugs, surgery, or physical interventions.

When my mom gave me the book a year prior I dismissed the idea. "I've seen my MRI," I had told her. "It shows a ruptured spinal disc that's clearly pressing against my spinal nerves! How can that NOT be causing my pain?"

But Dr. Sarno's work exposed a paradox: despite stunning medical advances, chronic pain is a worsening epidemic. In the U.S. over 100 million people suffer from chronic pain. Globally, it's 1.5 billion.[234] And current treatments offer minimal relief. There's little evidence that pain medications or physical treatments significantly improve quality of life or reduce chronic pain.[56] Even surgery is rarely beneficial, helping in only about one percent of lower back cases.[7] Mountains of research have shown that structural 'abnormalities' like herniated discs are common in asymptomatic individuals, and that brain-based treatments are extremely effective in eliminating pain.[8]

I was skeptical at first, but desperation had opened me up to anything. Dr. Sarno described the personality traits of people susceptible to chronic symptoms: people-pleasing, perfectionistic, worried, affected by low self-esteem. Especially susceptible were those going through stressful life events at the time of the onset.

I saw myself on every page. I realized how the stress of my first big pro race, on top of an existing cocktail of internalized pressure, was the perfect storm to create physical pain. I realized how my shifting symptoms couldn't be caused by that ruptured disc—that my back was 'normally abnormal'. I accepted that at some level my pain was my own invention—and it was up to me to dig myself out.

I followed Sarno's treatment program and within a few weeks, to my astonishment, I noticed a significant reduction in my pain levels. I started to drop my fear around sitting, riding my bike, and physical activities. Within a few weeks the low back pain that had plagued me for over two years was largely resolved. I couldn't believe it.

But then over the next year I experienced an array of other symptoms: pain and stiffness in my upper back, shin splints, knee pain, foot pain, quad stiffness, arm weakness. All generated by my brain, all would go away when I applied the Sarno methodology. But it felt like a never-ending loop. It was as if my brain was telling me that until I went inward and did the hard work I was going to continue playing whack-a-mole with these symptoms.

So I did. I enrolled with a therapist who specialized in brain-generated pain to get to the root causes of my internal pressure. I became deeply committed to a mindfulness practice. I realized how perfectionism was a survival mechanism to keep me from feeling that I wasn't good enough. I learned to approach my inner critic with compassion, not contempt.

Most importantly, I learned to feel my emotions.

IT WAS a tough journey but over time my symptoms, remarkably, started to dissipate. I returned to racing, but just because I could race again didn't mean I had to. Along with my back pain, my drive to become a professional had faded.

In the depths of my pain and suffering I would have given anything to be pain-free. And yet this experience was one of the best things to ever happen for me. The day before I was to leave for France to study abroad—a dream I never thought I'd accomplish because of my pain—I bawled with gratitude. I felt compassion for the younger Alec who had suffered so much. Awe for knowing that my body wasn't broken and in fact was stronger than I could have ever imagined. Pride for the payoff in my belief that someday things would change. I vowed to always remember that I am a powerful author of my story.

Years later, after leaving my job as a Manager at LinkedIn and teaming up with Scott Shute to create the first iteration of Changing Work, I started formal training to be a chronic pain elimination coach.

My calling is to empower millions to be pain free and to change the way the world sees and treats chronic pain—from 'pain management' to 'pain free.' I've been fortunate to play a role in remarkable recoveries like that of my first client, a chronic pain sufferer of thirty years who went from being unable to walk five minutes to doing half-marathons and all-day hikes, largely pain free.

My ruptured spinal disc is still there (confirmed on an MRI), but I've been free of back pain for over a decade and am unrestricted from any physical activity. What better proof for my clients that structural abnormalities don't always cause pain?

My journey was about overcoming chronic pain but it was also about something deeper.

We're told that if we get the right pill, procedure, or practitioner, that we'll be 'fixed'. In other words, we look for external solutions to internal problems. But we have innate wisdom and tools at our disposal, and if we learn to use them we won't just feel better, we'll connect to our own authenticity. We'll realize that we were, always have been, and always will be enough. That being ourselves brings others joy. That we can do what feels natural for us, not normal for society.

Put simply, my pain was a call inward to grow into an authentic, beautiful, joyous, and connected life.

I'm so glad I answered that call. And you can too.

From Pain Management to Pain Free

Alec Kassin

~

ALEC KASSIN is a former semi-professional cyclist and chronic back pain sufferer turned certified pain elimination coach for athletes. He is the Co-Founder of Pain Free Comeback, the first mind-body treatment program for athletes with chronic pain. Alec's mission is to change the way the world sees and treats chronic pain—from pain management to pain-free. He is a Founding Partner of Changing Work, former LinkedIn Manager, and graduate of UC Berkeley. Alec resides in Marin County, California.

---

1. Sarno, John E. *Healing back pain: The mind-body connection.* Balance, 2001.
2. Gereau IV, Robert W., et al. "A pain research agenda for the 21st century." *The Journal of Pain* 15.12 (2014): 1203-1214.
3. Goldberg, Daniel S., and Summer J. McGee. "Pain as a global public health priority." *BMC public health* 11 (2011): 1-5.
4. Zajacova, Anna, Hanna Grol-Prokopczyk, and Zachary Zimmer. "Pain trends among American adults, 2002–2018: patterns, disparities, and correlates." *Demography* 58.2 (2021): 711-738.
5. "Nice Recommends Range of Effective Treatments for People with Chronic Primary Pain and Calls on Healthcare Professionals to Recognise and Treat a Person's Pain as Valid and Unique to Them." *National Institute for Health and Care Excellence,* www.nice.org.uk/news/article/nice-recommends-range-of-effective-treatments-for-people-with-chronic-primary-pain-and-calls-on-healthcare-professionals-to-recognise-and-treat-a-person-s-pain-as-valid-and-unique-to-them. Accessed 13 May 2024.

6. Turk, Dennis C., Hilary D. Wilson, and Alex Cahana. "Treatment of chronic non-cancer pain." *The Lancet* 377.9784 (2011): 2226-2235.
7. United States Agency for Health Care Policy and Research. *Understanding Acute Low Back Problems*. U.S. Department of Health and Human Services, Public Health Service, Agency for Health Care Policy and Research, 1994. *Google Books*, www.books.google.fr/books?id=XKjSknrciGQC&printsec=frontcover&hl=fr&source=gbs_ge_summary_r&cad=0#v=onepage&q&f=false. Accessed 13 May 2024.
8. Ashar, Yoni K., et al. "Effect of pain reprocessing therapy vs placebo and usual care for patients with chronic back pain: a randomized clinical trial." *JAMA psychiatry* 79.1 (2022): 13-23.

EIGHTEEN

From Pink Slip to Inner Calm

Wendy McHenry

In July 2000 my then husband and I separated. I moved out abruptly, needing space. Our daughter was twenty months old. I remember grabbing the diaper bag, some clothes, the pack-n-play, and leaving while he was at work.

We eventually settled in a nice apartment a few blocks from my daughter's dad. I worked from home long before working remotely was cool, as my company was based back in Chicago. This was partly to take care of my daughter and partly because I had left Chicago for San Diego and the company seemed to like my work and asked me to stay onboard.

I filed for divorce in February 2001. I worked on the divorce paperwork Valentine's Day weekend, which had always been a special holiday for the two of us. We had been dating since September 1991, almost ten years together. Our divorce was final six months later and we had been married just under five years.

There was irony in the timing of it all. September 11, 2001, happened twenty days after our divorce was final. I was living in San Diego at the time and I remember uneasily watching the news that morning. I remember the shock of watching the plane hit the tower, that sinking feeling in my stomach. I remember holding my daughter close. I remember going to the bar where the Navy submariners liked to hang out, not fully grasping the gravity, how many of these military men would go fight in the upcoming war—how many would be lost.

On our home shores a new battle was brewing: the economic impact of 9/11.

In June 1999 my company, Market Facts, at which I had been working for two years, was acquired by another company, Synovate. I was a statistical analyst working primarily in market research consulting for consumer-packaged goods clients, brands you know and love. After 9/11 Synovate began shrinking the Market Facts team. Multiple rounds of layoffs were happening and I made it through a couple of rounds, getting more and more nervous.

Then finally, in January 2002, I received the dreaded phone call from my boss on a Friday afternoon. I was laid off.

I was laid off just a few weeks before my fifth employment anniversary when I would have been one hundred percent vested in my 401(k).

A numbness overtook me at the moment of that phone call. I didn't know what to do, where to go, who to tell, who to ask for help. I was dating someone (whom I later married) and he offered to take me out to the bar to drink my feelings, which is exactly what we did. We went to the Captains Quarters while my daughter was with her father and I drank until I didn't care. I had just lost my lifeline. I don't know what I was drinking but it probably had copious amounts of rum.

The only problem was, I woke up the next day and I had to be the one to do something about it. But what?

WE HAD MOVED to San Diego from Chicago for my ex-husband's postdoctoral research in 1999. Our move there was supposed to be temporary. I would go on to live in San Diego for eleven years, three years longer than my ex-husband.

But at the time I was laid off I found myself three thousand miles from home—from family, from friends—with a young child.

From Pink Slip to Inner Calm

She had just turned three. I was without a support network and without many options. My daughter's daycare was the best support network I had at the time, a perk of my ex-husband's job. She had been going to daycare only two days a week and was with me the rest of the time.

The severance package seemed generous at the time but ran out quickly. San Diego was—and still is—a very expensive city in which to live. I recall my 2002 rent being $1,650 a month for a two-bedroom, two-bathroom apartment in Point Loma, near the beach.

And as a budding statistician, most of the job postings in my field were for pharmaceutical or medical public health jobs and required a graduate degree I did not have.

I don't do well without a project to keep me focused and busy. I only made it two weeks without work before I had to jump into action. I decided to audit some classes in statistics at San Diego State University while I worked on my applications for jobs and to see if I could get into graduate school. This included working on the requirements for different graduate programs. I had never taken the GRE and quickly got that scheduled, and after attaining a perfect score I started my Master's degree.

Although in the spring semester of 2003 I began work as a graduate teaching associate with an annual stipend of $10,000, by this time I had already spent my severance and my savings. I was charging groceries and gas on my credit card and not paying it off, because every dollar I had scraped together was going to my rent. I wasn't getting any alimony or child support either, because as a postdoctoral researcher my ex-husband wasn't making much more than I was.

The financial situation was becoming more and more dire. I lived near the San Diego Department of Public Health and I made an appointment for assistance through the Women, Infants, and Children (WIC) nutrition assistance program for families with little ones under the age of five. This program allowed me to access fresh fruits and vegetables, whole grains, milk, eggs, bread, cereal, juice, peanut butter, soy milk, tofu and more, through grocery coupons.

I was grateful, but with those coupons I knew that everyone

could see I was receiving government assistance.

I felt so much embarrassment and shame. I could feel the weight of others' judgment. I felt shame each time I walked into the Public Health Clinic. I felt like those coupons were screaming out that I was a bad mother, when instead I should have been proud that I was doing what I needed to do to take care of my child. My then boyfriend would tease me and tell me we were eating "government cheese".

But his words were nothing compared to the words I told myself, and which I told myself for years.

I shamed myself for getting into this position in the first place. I didn't understand at the time that the job loss was not my fault and had nothing to do with my actual performance.

I didn't start a full-time job again until May of 2004, more than two years after I was laid off. I didn't even graduate with the Master's degree, I had to go back to work. Between raising my child and working, I never finished my Master's thesis—something else that filled me with shame and disappointment in myself. Instead I should be proud of how hard I have worked. I have ended up having an incredible career. I am truly blessed with the many gifts I have been given.

But because of this experience, I have spent years in therapy unraveling the emotions.

The experience of losing my job worsened a predisposition for anxiety and depression.

The experience of losing my job left me with a deep-seated sense of shame, thinking (erroneously) that somehow it was my fault.

The experience of losing my job left me with financial insecurity, feeling like I never had enough and constantly feeling worried about losing my job.

The experience of losing my job left me with a tendency to overwork, even today, and especially since the pandemic-era layoffs we have all experienced, I throw all of myself into my career and I struggle to find a healthy work-life balance.

. . .

IN JANUARY 2023, the tech industry began laying off sales talent in droves. Through my work in our industry group, the PreSales Collective, I have met dozens upon dozens of professionals who were impacted by layoffs.

Between my experience being laid off and in meeting with others more recently affected by wide-scale employment changes, here is what I recommend if you find yourself in this position.

First, give yourself time to process your emotions before you dive back in to a job search. Some people are angry, some are sad, some are relieved. If you are experiencing extreme emotions, please seek out support, whether it be family, friends, or a licensed therapist. If your previous company provides it, take advantage of employee assistance program support to meet with a therapist. I have spent a great deal of time in therapy processing what happened, and I find it helpful to this day to help me cope with the demands of a stressful job.

If you begin your job search too soon, these extreme emotions will show up and be apparent to recruiters and hiring managers. It's best to wait until your emotions have calmed. Some people are ready in a few days, but I have known others who needed a month or more to begin their job search anew.

Second, if your previous employer offered career services, utilize and take advantage of them. From updating your resume and LinkedIn to practicing interviewing skills, career services and career coaches can provide invaluable guidance.

Third, and I know you are probably tired of hearing this, but utilizing your network is extremely important in today's job market. Hiring managers are inundated with applicants, and you absolutely need to find ways to stand out.

Fourth, and perhaps most importantly, I highly recommend taking the time for self-care. If you didn't previously have a good self-care routine, this is the time to start one. Things I have tried that have helped me include building a daily meditation practice and a daily walk outside in nature. Also taking time to get together with family or with friends. Find those things that bring you joy and that nurture you, and make them a daily priority. Consistency is what has helped me the most—I show up and take time for my self-care no matter how I am feeling that day. If you find yourself struggling with depression or anxiety during this time, self-care can help you keep a good baseline. If you can do so, a therapist can help you manage these emotions during this stressful time.

No matter what, it's very important to understand that the layoff was not your fault and was not related to your job performance or to your self-worth. I have seen some extremely high performers impacted by layoffs and it is critical to keep this at the top of your mind. It feels deeply personal I know, and this is what I think is hardest about a job layoff.

Job changes are typically a time of self-reflection. I have seen some candidates entirely switch their career path. I have seen some candidates leave the tech industry completely. I have seen others invest in what was previously a side project. I have seen some impressive athletic feats undertaken with the extra time available. I have seen some candidates travel the world during this time and I have seen some candidates utilize the experience to take an early retirement.

Whatever path you decide, taking care of your mental health is of paramount importance. During your career search, taking care of your mental health is just as important as networking, updating your resume, and applying to jobs. It will help you manage the emotions of the stress you are undergoing and it will help you show up as your best self when you are interviewing. It will ultimately bring you more success in your job search.

Remember, most people land better jobs than the ones they were in before, jobs that align more with their calling and with what their heart wants.

So once you've landed your dream job (and you will), lift someone else up. Help another person with their job search, make an introduction, offer a reference if that is relevant.

If I've learned anything, it's that together we are professionals who can give meaning and purpose to what we do for a living.

Wendy McHenry

∼

WENDY MCHENRY is currently the Global Head of Solutions Engineering at CData Software in Chapel Hill, North Carolina. Across an almost thirty-year career in consulting, analytics, and technology, she has led technical teams across several countries spanning different global regions. Wendy has always taken an active approach to mentoring and developing tech talent at all stages of their career growth. She is a fierce inclusionist, advocating for diversity of viewpoints and backgrounds, and currently serves as Chairperson of the PreSales Collective Women in Solutions Excellence Council. Additionally, Wendy currently serves on the board of two nonprofit organizations in her community.

NINETEEN

From Panic Attacks to Self-Discovery
Matt McLaughlin

In 1999 the world was abuzz with the promise of the Internet, a digital landscape ripe with opportunity and innovation. For many, including myself, this promise represented not just a career change but a seismic shift in how we perceived work, success, and our place in a rapidly-evolving digital era.

I vividly remember the exhilaration of being swept up in the currents of the dot-com boom. It was a time of boundless optimism, where possibilities seemed limitless and dreams felt within reach. Landing a director-level position at a well-funded internet start-up felt like winning the golden ticket, a validation of my skills and potential. The sudden doubling of my salary was not just a financial windfall but a confirmation that I was on the right path and that my interest in digital marketing was valued and sought after.

However, as quickly as the euphoria of success washed over me, so too did the harsh reality of the challenges ahead. The departure of seasoned marketing veterans left a gaping void and put me in a position of leadership and responsibility for which I felt ill-prepared. Despite my proficiency in digital marketing tactics the weight of managing an entire marketing strategy felt like an anchor dragging me down into unplumbed waters.

Self-doubt became my constant companion, a nagging voice whispered insidious thoughts of inadequacy and fear of failure. The once-exciting prospect of steering the company's marketing efforts now loomed before me like an insurmountable mountain, casting a shadow over my confidence and competence. The pressure to deliver results and justify my new-found position gnawed at me and threatened to unravel the seemingly fragile framework of success that I had so painstakingly built.

With each passing day the grip of anxiety tightened its hold, clouding my thoughts with irrational fears. The thought of losing everything I had worked so hard to achieve haunted my every waking moment, a relentless specter that refused to be ignored. Sleep became an elusive luxury as worry and apprehension invaded even the sanctuary of my dreams, leaving me exhausted and depleted.

The once-thriving energy of the start-up environment now felt suffocating. Its toxic culture exacerbated my already fragile state of mind. Long hours and constant pressure only compounded my anxiety and pushed me further into a downward spiral of despair. Panic attacks became a cruel manifestation of my inner turmoil and rendered me powerless in the face of overwhelming stress.

Despite my best efforts to conceal my struggles the cracks began to show. The trust and confidence of those around me eroded. My inability to make decisions and my penchant for avoidance only served to undermine my credibility as a leader, further isolating me in my sea of uncertainty.

In the end it wasn't just my career that suffered under the weight of my anxiety—it was my health, my relationships, and my sense of self-worth. The once-promising trajectory of my career had veered off course and I was left grappling with feelings of inadequacy.

I EVENTUALLY FOUND a way out of my crippling imposter syndrome by learning to look at my thoughts objectively. My introduction to mindfulness practice led to a decades-long study of meditation and cognitive behavioral therapy. Over several months I slowly pulled myself out of the darkness and began to see a way forward.

One of the beliefs I learned to question was that I'd never find another job that paid this well again. I took a small step forward and simply started looking at job postings. By identifying this belief and questioning it, I saw many more opportunities than I ever would have thought. I also challenged the idea that I lacked extensive expertise in my role as a digital marketer. In truth nobody had extensive experience in the field back then. In 1999 Google celebrated its first birthday; the first online transaction occurred only five years before that.

As I began to unravel these assumptions I also began training my mind to remain present and impartial to turbulent thoughts and emotions. While they didn't disappear, I gained distance and objectivity from them. Soon after that, a very empowering shift happened. I realized that I did have a large degree of control over my circumstances. The toxic high-pressure culture revealed itself as an unnecessary burden and in a sudden revelatory moment I resigned without a new position lined up. While the anxious thoughts were still there I also entertained the possibility of finding a better role in a company with a supportive culture. Within two weeks I accepted a role that paid even more, without the stress and toxic culture.

Looking back, I can see how my thoughts and assumptions of how things should be, drove me into a state of anxiety and panic. Where before I felt out of depth, I now see it as a challenge that I could have readily accepted.

NO ONE ever starts anything new without some degree of uncertainty. In fact anxiety can often be a sign that we're in a place of growth. Realizing this, and that anxiety is a natural part of any new endeavor, is a huge shift in how I look at taking on new challenges.

In so many ways I was trying to live up to expectations that were unrealistic and unfounded—maintaining a new house in perfect order, being successful in a new role, navigating a toxic culture that was totally out of my control. I also found a way forward with my studies in mindfulness and cognitive behavioral therapy. I began to study Buddhism in earnest and learned a great deal about myself and how our assumptions and thoughts can take over without us even knowing. Some twenty-five years later these panic attacks have receded into distant memory. And while I still live with some anxiety, I think that's normal and part of life. I've come to accept that, and have built up several habits and practices that allow me continued growth and development.

First among these practices is mindfulness. A simple breathing meditation invites us to focus on the breath, and when our mind wanders to gently bring our attention back to the breath. Over time, we develop the ability to watch our thoughts and emotions like a movie screen. We notice that our thoughts change, arise, disappear, and vary in strength and frequency. They are not permanent, and are not a fixed part of ourselves. In fact we eventually discover a part of our mind that can watch the thoughts impartially and can actually choose to become engaged in them, or not.

A profound saying, attributed to many teachers over the centuries, sums up this experience: We don't have to believe everything we think. From this perspective we notice patterns of thoughts or repeating themes that we can identify. To practice this meditation, follow these steps.

1. Find a comfortable position, sitting or lying down. You can use a cushion or chair to support your posture. Keep your spine erect but not rigid, allowing for natural alignment.
2. Relax your body: close your eyes gently and bring your attention to your body. Take a few deep breaths, let go of any tension or tightness with each exhalation. Soften your facial muscles, shoulders, and any other areas of tension.
3. Focus on the breath: notice the sensation of the air entering and leaving your nostrils or the rise and fall of

your chest or abdomen. Choose one point of focus and anchor your awareness there.
4. Be present: as you breathe in and out, simply observe the breath without trying to control it. Notice the rhythm, texture, and quality of each breath. If your mind wanders, gently guide it back to the breath without judgment.
5. Stay with the sensation: remain fully present with each inhalation and exhalation, moment by moment. Let go of thoughts about the past or future, allow yourself to immerse in the present experience of breathing fully.
6. Practice non-attachment: if distractions arise—thoughts, emotions, or bodily sensations—acknowledge them with kindness and let them pass without engagement. Return your focus to the breath.
7. End with gratitude: after a few minutes or as long as you wish, gradually bring your awareness back to your surroundings. Take a moment to appreciate this time you've dedicated to your well-being.

After the meditation, reflect on any recurring thoughts that came up, particularly the challenging ones. Once we identify these thoughts, we can start to work with them.

Let's use an example of a thought that I struggled with: "I'll never get another job that pays this well again."

A first impulse could involve trying to get rid of the thought as though we could banish it to some dark forgotten corner of our mind. This might work in the short term but over time we find ourselves spending a ton of energy stuffing that thought down and trying to run from it. At this point the thought still has power over us. Instead we can accept the thought. In this example, it is entirely in the realm of possibility that I would never find a job that pays that well. We can even thank that part of our mind for pointing out the potential danger. The key here is to look at additional possibilities. That worst-case scenario lies within the realm of possibility, but what else could happen?

Now is the time to ask ourselves three questions:

1. What is the best-case scenario? In our example, I might (and did!) find an even better-paying job with a much better culture.
2. What is the most likely scenario? I might be out of work for a while and I might not find the perfect job at first, but I'll probably find something that pays the bills for now.
3. If the worst-case scenario happened, would I survive? Let's assume that I would never find a job that paid that well again. So what? I'd survive, my family would survive, we'd figure out a way to pay the bills and life would go on. Absolute worst case, we'd sell the house. That's not a desirable outcome, but it's also not commensurate with the agony of debilitating panic attacks, which are a self-defense mechanism designed to help us fight or run for our lives.

With these other possibilities to consider, we notice that catastrophic thinking holds less power over us. Other outcomes exist, some even more likely than the ones we fear most.

Next, we put our two practices together.

With our mindfulness practice we can notice when our catastrophic thinking ramps up. Using our ability to notice the thought and redirect it, we remind ourselves of the three questions above. We now have a gap between the stimulus (the catastrophic thinking) and the response (how we choose to focus our attention). We simply shift from attention on the breath to attention on the three questions.

From the depths of imposter-syndrome-induced anxiety to leading with confidence, for me this journey enabled growth and self-discovery. Despite grappling with self-doubt and fear of failure, I emerged stronger and more resilient, armed with new-found insights and coping mechanisms.

Through mindfulness practice and cognitive behavioral therapy

I learned to navigate the turbulent waters of uncertainty with grace and equanimity. By challenging ingrained assumptions and embracing the present moment, I liberated myself from the shackles of catastrophic thinking and reclaimed control over my career.

The pivotal decision to prioritize my well-being and seek out a supportive work environment proved transformative; it led to newfound opportunities and personal fulfillment.

As I reflect on my journey I am reminded that adversity often serves as a catalyst for growth. It pushes us to confront our inner demons and emerge stronger on the other side. With mindfulness, self-awareness, and cognitive behavioral therapy techniques in my toolbox, I'm actually grateful for my journey as it has enabled me to achieve my goals and to help others through this process.

MATT MCLAUGHLIN

Matt McLaughlin

~

MATT MCLAUGHLIN has over twenty-five years of experience building high-performance teams and leaders. With specialties in fostering emotional intelligence, self-awareness, and communication skills, Matt helps CEOs, founders, managers, and leaders increase their impact on people, planet, and profit. Matt has experience in a wide range of industries including non-profits, high-tech, pharmaceuticals, consumer packaged goods, healthcare, education, manufacturing, government, and finance. From new managers to tenured CEOs, Matt partners with leaders of all levels to achieve their full potential.

TWENTY

Feel The Burn

Désirée Pascual & Jill Santercier

Urban legend has it that if you place a frog in a pot of boiling water it will instantly leap out. When the water is pleasantly tepid but gradually heated up, the frog will remain in the water, oblivious until it is too late. It is difficult to pinpoint when I transitioned from tepid to searing, likely because it was such a gradual process.

All I know is that one night, after a restless three hours of trying to quiet my mind enough to finally drift off to sleep, I woke abruptly a short time later, terrified, unable to move or think clearly, paralyzed by anxiety and crippling physical pain. In the terrifying darkness of my room, I frantically scrambled for any shred of control—the reassuring contours of my bed, the sturdy angles of the armoire, the familiar creaking of a settling house—desperate for a lifeline to re-tether me to a familiar reality. As I lay there, bartering for assurance that I would fight my way back as I'd always done, I realized that none of the well-worn life preservers—sheer willpower, dogged tenacity, stubborn rationalization—would save me this time. With each passing moment the darkness claimed me more completely, dragged me into an uncompromising sadness that would last for months.

"Burnout," my physician summarized after several tests and visits.

"How?" I asked incredulously. "Can this happen doing work that I love?"

"You're not alone," she responded matter-of-factly, shrugging her shoulders. "It's rampant and we have seen a huge uptick during- and post-pandemic. Burnout happens gradually, sometimes over the course of a couple of years and recovery follows roughly the same timeline. There is no magic quick-fix. You cannot self-care your way out of burnout."

While self-care practices undoubtedly hold value in nurturing one's well-being, they alone cannot extinguish the searing, full-bodied impact of burnout. With its insidious grip, burnout extends far beyond the comforts of bubble baths and meditation sessions. Adrift from ourselves, neither physicians nor mental health staff are able to accelerate the recovery process of an utterly abandoned body, mind, and soul.

LIFE OFTEN SHOWS itself in authentically tragic variations before we grow responsive to its cues to pause and reflect. Retracing our journey takes time. It requires the courage to feel the distance between our innermost values and the unvarnished reality within which we now exist.

Doing work we love requires vigilance. To be fueled without discernment by promises of purpose and impact makes us prone to self-sacrifice, and puts us at risk of exploitation. This purpose-driven workaholism is also a surprisingly effective distraction from all kinds of feelings and can therefore be noxiously self-serving. A soul hungry for meaning and approval will do almost anything to get them. But an insatiable quest for professional recognition and status has less to do with material comfort than with a yearning for belonging. Burnout, then, is not merely a state of physical exhaustion, it's a profound existential crisis writ large in the narrative of our lives.

Current data paints a disturbing picture. In 2022, 86% of

remote workers and 70% of in-person workers reported being burnt out.[1] In 2023 mid-level manager burnout rose to 53%.[2] The effects are viral and trickle down to families and loved ones. A 2024 survey found that 71% of employees report that work stress has caused a personal relationship to end; 39% of employees report that work has negatively impacted their ability to care for their family.[3]

The pandemic-related large-scale transition of how work gets done has led to "always on" cultures—longer hours and heavily blurred boundaries between personal and professional lives. Affecting employees and leaders alike, these statistics are the by-product of an era defined by relentless corporate ambition, wherein success is measured in metrics and milestones and the pursuit of purpose and meaning can lead us down paths toxically misaligned with our innermost values and longing.

However unpalatable, many come to accept this sense of misalignment with passive resignation. This gradual acquiescence is fed by the sheer authority that corporations reflect by their existence, power, and finely tuned communications engines. We find ourselves asking, 'Is it me? Do I lack the resilience, grit, or intelligence to be a meaningful part of this?'

This inquiry is a deeply flawed but prevalent response to burnout. In fact it is neither personal weakness nor a lack of resilience that breaks us. It is not hard work that leaves us depleted. Rather it is relentless, unfocused, non-sequitur work, in pursuit of corporate goals that are often opaque, ever-shifting, or utterly misaligned with our values—that crushes our souls.

Burning the candle at both ends, we move ahead fiercely to evade each sign of the crevasse that separates us from our lives. The heroic hustle narrative lends us the dignity we need to keep going. We do not merely summon the effort to continue on from a place of bravery, we reason that if we keep hustling perhaps we can escape the threat of uncertainty and insignificance by creating the space for others to see and appreciate us. Underscored by recurring mass layoffs, psychological safety and the social contract between employee and employer continue to erode, leaving employees feeling scared and disillusioned. Our ceaseless hustle then is often nothing more than a plea for safety within poorly managed ecosystems.

Burnout is different from stress. Stress can be invigorating and fuel high achievement while chronic toxic stress can make us sick. Burnout topples us. It is the kill switch we failed to push. We enter an altered state in which our body collapses. This freezing response serves as a last-ditch survival strategy for a person who has ignored every red flag and depleted all resources. The trauma often lingers long after the recovery period and can later show up as post-traumatic stress.

FORTUNATELY, a body in crisis takes on a life of its own, overriding our drive to function, contort, and rationalize.

Frightening as it may seem, burnout is a life-saving call to pause and turn inward so that we might eventually find our way back to our center—the very place from where we are infinite in our potential to do our best and most meaningful work.

The good news is that one of the causes of both happiness and misery is the quality of the environments within which we choose to exist. Knowing this reintroduces choice, and choice invites agency: we are free to explore the inner landscape that led us to the boiling point, arguably the most important thing we can—and must—do to pivot and weave a new story. We can leave in search of a more values-aligned environment, or choose to craft our own. We can stay and choose to direct our efforts toward advocating for systemic change. Or we can stay and simply reframe our relationship to work. Or we can do any combination of these. We cannot control nor bend an environment to fit our unique needs, nor should we distort ourselves to fit into an environment that feels unsafe. But we can pause, get curious, and explore our options. **The first and arguably most difficult part of our journey toward recovery is a brutally honest look at where we find ourselves.** Here we are, standing at the jagged edge of a cliff with a long drop down into the unknown. The terrifying, searing heat of burnout that threatens to consume us has mercilessly pushed us toward this edge. With our body, mind, and soul in shambles, there is nothing to hold onto.

Rather than being pushed and pulled by external forces that sever us from our core, we must gradually surrender to a period of radical rest by first returning to our breath and then to our five senses. There is a betrayal of the body that precedes the crash of burnout. Changing course requires that we rebuild trust with our Self. With support, we can begin to reclaim those deeply intimate moments when we felt completely safe and at home in ourselves: *I have survived. I can claim space to disconnect, rest, breathe, and be. I have agency. I am safe here. I can trust... me.*

From this place of safety we can begin to examine our relationship to work. What is the impetus for our complicity against our better judgment? What do we need? By articulating our yearning, we gain a better perspective. No judgment, no blame—both of which only exacerbate stress and maladaptive coping strategies. Once we embrace our unique vulnerabilities we can step back and examine them with greater curiosity and objectivity. The gift in this process is that external validation gradually becomes less important. In examining our pain we no longer need to resort to unproductive externally focused behaviors in order to silence it. From this new and more objective perch we might find that we are triggered by a coworker or manager who mimics the behavior of a dysfunctional family dynamic. We may discover that we project old power dynamics upon new environments, which renders us stuck in dissonant, exhausting, and unproductive fight, flight, or freeze responses. Whatever we find—and face—becomes pliable. We can change it. Insight frees us from misplaced resentment, projection, and the pressure to perform to exhaustion for the wrong reasons. It is a slow and deliberate process of deconstructing triggers and reclaiming our power.

Finally, we can reflect on whether or not work is objectively too demanding or values-misaligned. If we find this to be true we can revisit whether or not we need to signal stronger boundaries, or leave. Rituals can be helpful in structuring well-boundaried workdays: a mid-day walk with the dog, blocked time for meditation or prayer, or rituals that signal that the workday has ended. There will always be more work to do yet our time and energy are finite. Protecting these rituals and boundaries with poignancy and rigor provides us with freedom: to breathe, to just be, to explore the complexities and mysteries of our lives and the world around us, to once again belong to ourselves first.

BURNOUT IS MOST OFTEN WHOLLY avoidable if leaders structure business priorities mindfully, placing the human at the center of their strategies.

A culture of urgency discerningly focuses on the most important things. But an immature, always-on hustle culture indiscriminately labels everything as urgent and leaves substantial human collateral in its wake. The indiscriminate grind renders the worker fragmented and feeling as though their work is inconsequential, which in turn inflicts substantial moral injury as it refutes purpose-driven mission statements. This dissonance is a fast-track to burnout. To expect optimal team performance amidst a chaotic and misaligned work environment is as absurd as expecting a race car to win a race while fueled by water. When companies prioritize profits over people, unconscious leaders create perilous and harmful cultures.

Self-aware emotionally intelligent leaders understand that building sustainable and profitable enterprises requires equal measures of focused human-centered strategy, deep operational acumen, values-congruent purposeful action, *and* heart. The lifespan of the corporate unicorn, unlike that of its mythical counterpart, can be cut painfully short if business leaders disregard the inalienable truth that it is humans—their creativity, depth, dynamism, and adaptability—who are the heartbeat of an organization. Their energy is finite and optimal performance requires a balance between focused, purposeful urgency, and rest. It follows then that corporate hygiene is one of the single most important factors in preventing burnout and positioning teams and organizations to succeed. When we create the conditions for people to thrive, an organization's bottom line does too.

Feel The Burn

During and after the pandemic many mid-level managers and leaders felt like unnetted trapeze artists, unsure and unsupported as they navigated rapid change and unfamiliar terrain. This unprecedented crisis taught us that during times of disruption it is not about having all of the answers, but about showing up with humility, curiosity, compassion, and deep resolve grounded in shared values. This rings as true for our organizations as it does in our personal lives.

Emotionally charged work environments require self-aware, grounded leadership, rather than untethered, reactive busyness fueled by bravado, greed, or status anxiety. Authentic connection to ourselves and the people we lead are the anchors that alert high-impact leaders when to slow down, pause, and re-focus. Fully understanding the effects of toxic stress, burnout, and its consequences, is the barometer that must inform the corporate temperature dial.

Life and work are full of surprises. Our quest for happiness sometimes leads us to the unlikeliest of places. That night, trapped in a paralyzed body in the darkness of my bedroom, I was brought to my knees, bewildered, grieving, raging against my frailty. Yet absolute and uncompromising surrender, once my most dreaded nemesis, led me to discover that curiosity, self-awareness, and compassion toward self and others, can restore and catapult us—and the organizations we lead—to unimagined heights.

No burning required.

Désirée Pascual & Jill Santercier

∼

DÉSIRÉE PASCUAL and **JILL SANTERCIER,** co-founders of Simply Human, are innovative, human-centered HR strategists who enable businesses of all sizes and industries to achieve peak performance and dynamic engagement. They believe that cutting-edge differentiation is uncovered along roads less traveled. Drawing on insights from behavioral sciences, data analytics, and decades of in-the-trenches HR leadership, their visionary client-specific solutions have helped organizations transform into vibrant workplaces that unleash their full potential through—and with—people.

---

1. International Labour Office. *Working anytime, anywhere: The effects on the world of work.* Publications Office of the European Union, 2022.
2. Klinghoffer, Dawn, and Kirkpatrick-Husk, Katie. "More Than 50% of Managers Feel Burned Out." *HBR*, May 18, 2023.
3. Headspace. *Workforce State of Mind Report.* Author, 2024.

Opening to Wonder

TWENTY-ONE

Pasta Poetica

Emma Laurence

I'm standing in the pasta aisle at my local grocery store, staring at a shoreline of blue boxes with little clear plastic windows, wondering which shape to buy. My favorite, fusilli, the one that (let's be honest) holds the sauce best, is too clunky for this project. I admit I'm a creative person. But in this moment I sigh, questioning how a coveted teaching job at one of the top prep schools in the country has been reduced to macaroni.

When our school year began, my department chair delivered the news in a kindly manner: due to production rotations in various campus performance spaces, this year I'd be directing the middle school production in the upper division theater. Was I okay with that?

I'm sorry, what?

Gross Theater is a 630-seat Broadway-style venue. It's the crown jewel performance space in a world where geniuses are groomed for Ivy League colleges and elite leaders begin their training.

The image of thirty-five-plus full-throttle pubescents on the main stage flashes in my consciousness as I blink rapidly. I recover quickly—$10,000 of actor training kicking in—and assure him that of course we can do this—a great learning experience for the kids, no worries that it has to be a straight play rather than a musical that would at least include big song and dance numbers to cover the whole space!

Last time we tried tweens in Gross Theater our set designer wisely suggested placing the audience on stage in risers to surround three quarters of the playing space. Brilliant. Perfect for a parody the kids wrote on their adolescent experience: "Take a Look at Yourself and Laugh." But am I laughing now? No. Because there's a reason the average burnout rate for middle school teachers is three years. We love them, we do. It's just that keeping up with their physical, social, and emotional growth outpaces us. Our New York City seventh graders should be shipped to the Midwest to farm the land for a year. They might return more appreciative of our adult-designed classroom learning. Or simply never come back. This time, I have to crack the code on using the whole stage.

For me the sheer panic of directing middle schoolers in a huge space came down to a simple skill, one I lacked. I knew how to choose material carefully. I'd always been great at casting (my directing teacher, Mike Nichols, used to say that that was 90% of his films' success) and coaching actors. I love to honor the story and achieve artistry through vision and collaboration. But ask me to do the simplest task of imagining blocking (stage movement) in advance in my head? Yikes. With older actors I could show up at rehearsals with general staging ideas and we'd finesse details together, sculpting the space based on character, story, and stage picture. With middle schoolers on an expansive stage I'd have to be prepared with entrances and exits, clarity on each character's physical arc, and a flow that both students could follow and audiences would enjoy watching.

Enter the macaroni. I'd heard about a director who used pieces of pasta on his kitchen table to simulate movement of actors. Shifting the pieces around helped him imagine the best spot for characters in each scene and an overall visual throughline. That did make me laugh, and I was desperate enough to try it.

Back at the supermarket I choose elbows. I figure they're big enough to work with yet small enough to block a full-cast crowd scene. Once home, I clear the kitchen table, lay down the poster board where I'd sketched our theater parameters to scale, and pour some pasta into a bowl.

I love that clinking sound of uncooked macaroni hitting ceramic. Cool. Now what?

Surprising progress

I DECIDE to start with the top of the show and work one scene at a time. It's unbelievably slow. The set design of large block platforms creates three levels, meaning I'll have vertical as well as horizontal choices to make. The smallest platform is on wheels, detachable from the largest one. Only a few props needed, and the performers' imagination brings to life a wide-open landscape, a river, a schoolhouse, a raft, a barn. Our imagination ignites theirs. If I see where the actors go, they can communicate the story. Some people have this 3D imaging gift naturally. I do not. I have to work for that. But my only option is playful persistence in a new skill, a new area, a new way.

Once working with the pasta, I find that my intuition kicks in. I knew to anchor the banjo player and fiddler in one spot whenever they appeared. I'm inspired to have the schoolchildren enter left and skip across the entire stage for their "walk to school". As I stand up and take a deep breath hovering over the big picture, I'm surprised that my inner vision begins to shift to seeing actors rather than elbows. I see Tom and Huck stand on the tallest platform surveying their domain. I imagine Injun Joe unhooking the detachable block in slow motion, pushing it downstage as if launching the raft downriver at the end of Act I. I'm starting to get the hang of this! I realize the pasta is a playful prompt. It brings forward gifts I have, but haven't fully realized. Seeing *The Adventures of Tom Sawyer* unfold becomes like a dance on the main stage. It's everything I'd wished for—a chance to bring to life the swirl of an iconic American tale.

Cast, crew, and audience

PROCEEDING SLOWLY AND CAREFULLY, I draw a schema of what I envision—one page per scene—to bring to rehearsal. I trace each character's arc, writing their initials at their entrance and exit points. This way each actor can see his or her particular throughline amidst the many. Those drawings proved invaluable! After our full cast warm up, actors rehearsing the upcoming scene would gather round and I'd take them through their "marks" on the page.

They loved it. Not only did these smart, devoted student actors commit to lines, blocking, and character, they caught the energy of the artistic flow. They brought their very best to that larger dance. The pasta technique provided me with a platform of communication I hadn't known before, one that proved perfectly suited to orchestrating middle schoolers. And while they leaned into the macaroni-inspired maps I leaned into my calm center, the inner space I needed to lead our performance process in a state of remarkable order and beauty.

The results astounded me. My department chair called it the best middle school production in twenty years. The head of the middle division approached me after a performance, misty-eyed. One of my closest colleagues said something that took me totally by surprise: "That had you written all over it." And that was the moment I learned, without being able to put it into words, how true artistry is created.

A creative roadmap

I COULDN'T HAVE TOLD you what landed in my heart during the run of *The Adventures of Tom Sawyer*. Only now do I see the unfolding of a major turning point in self-awareness, in my understanding of artistry and leadership. Revelations about self-love, communication, and structure provide a blueprint today for how I live in creativity and collaboration with others. It starts with me, as a leader, knowing myself and accepting responsibility with confidence and humility.

I learned that my most impactful gifts are communicated without words. Yes, playwrights use words. We all use words every day. But it's the intention, the love, the vision behind the words that's communicated to others—be they actors, audience, co-workers, families, or strangers on the street. We're always sending out message-waves like a broadcast tower. And as we contribute to any kind of project, team, or performance, our personal vibrational signature reaches through to communicate. Our actions and choices are powerful transmitters.

In choosing to embrace the pasta technique I set in motion a whole series of effects. The first was to calm my own fear by addressing my lack of skill in a playful way. When a challenge beckons me beyond my limitations, pushing me into discomfort, I need to trust my ability to adapt to a new and bigger stage. How? The most simple, quirky, fun, silly, out-of-the-box, or unconventional approach is what motivates me from self-judgment into a playful place. Play relaxes my heart, eases the pressure, and I slow down. I start to ground in my calm (and often comedic) core, and practice patience to learn a new skill. I can allow myself grace to learn while I lead; that's OK. Leaning into structure, the best practical tool to share an overarching vision, I can rest assured that what I don't yet know *is* the open space into which creativity lands.

I learned to persist in this process, to take my time to do the work that communicates the vision to my team. In *Tom Sawyer*, the drawings made all the difference in bringing calm, beauty, and order to rehearsals, allowing actors to confidently ground in themselves and their talents. While protecting and anchoring me, the schemata gave my team a clear, measured approach to the production's mechanics. This gave the cast artistic as well as physical room to breathe, expand and fill the big space, just as I had expanded my inner vision when standing over the kitchen table. I became my best artist-director-facilitator with these kids. They became free to express their best actor-character-contributor. From the pasta came the poetry. It's structure that supports a successful work of art.

In my creative work today, my voice teacher is always reminding me: "From the small comes the big." The principle applies to singing the highest notes in my register, a technique of focusing the sound to a single point at the bridge of the nose. For years I had no desire to be classically trained. Now I find that specific, practical, and full-body awareness of my instrument is what creates the artistry when I sing jazz and pop. Consistent practices ground me, giving me the best shot to rise high in performance. Technique provides structure for art to flow through with clarity, energy, grace, and joy.

Leading to the level of artistry

OVER TIME, I've gained the confidence that no matter what comes my way I'll eventually turn the experience into a work of art. I've been tested on this point multiple times and in ways I never could have predicted. I've had to learn to own every challenge, every large or small leadership role, with all their responsibilities and rewards. Creativity is what continues to help me grow into expanding roles.

What if we, as self-aware leaders, elevate what we offer in the classroom, the boardroom, the Zoom-room to a work of art? I believe others are waiting for us to make it easier for them to bring their best.

As we pay attention to what our team, our family, or our community most needs, can we step up to that new stage with a sense of play, trusting the structure to hold us? As we widen and deepen our capacity to hold a higher vision, we tend to the creativity within ourselves and open up new realities and bring them into being.

And what if we're open to the one simple, silly skill that will allow those around us to relax, to expand, and bring their best? We may be surprised at how the small leads to the big.

Leadership is a big responsibility, especially as our broadcast area expands. Thoughts and choices matter. So let's play. Let's give ourselves the grace we would show to the one we love most. And let's create works of art together through structure, communication, and persistence.

Pasta Poetica

Emma Laurence

~

EMMA LAURENCE, CLC, is the founder of Life is Coaching You, author of the *Beyond Burnout Playbook*, and lead singer for JazzLove. Her NYC background as an award-winning actress, director, singer, and teacher brings dynamic creativity to coaching life-work transitions, mentoring millennial leaders from Fortune 100 companies, innovative small businesses, the arts and academia. Her blog, Living As Music, explores the power of sound to awaken self-awareness and expand consciousness, thereby raising leadership to a work of art.

TWENTY-TWO

Choose Your Story

Tim Van Ness

Sitting behind her mahogany desk in a big red leather wing-tipped chair, the Dean of the College of Music smiles and says, "So Tim, what do you think of our campus?"

I'm stumped. I feel lost, unsettled, nervous. After three years at three different colleges I'm in the midst of a "gap year", auditioning nationwide to figure out where I *really* want to study music education and theatre. On paper, this school, the University of Northern Colorado (UNC), has a very good music ed program. But here at its Greeley campus, with its plain ugly buildings smelling of cow shit surrounded by flat farmland, the mountains I'd hoped for are barely visible on the horizon.

My job here is to make a good impression and secure this school as a viable option. But I'm not quite sure how to answer her question.

"Well..." I start tentatively, concerned about offending her.

"Trust that!" she says interrupting me.

"Excuse me?"

"Trust yourself. Trust that response. I can see you're a transfer student, that you're coming from San Francisco and upstate New York before that. We have a very good program here, but this place is not for everyone. If you're not happy here on campus, it will impact you academically, musically, and possibly the rest of your life. You need to be sure you know this is where you want to be."

Crap. I have to agree. What now? What a big waste of a trip, time, money. Hmmm.

I hear Boulder is a cool town, and home to the University of Colorado, only sixty-four miles down the highway. A few hours later I arrive there, a completely different scene: a gorgeous campus with beautiful southwestern architecture on the edge of the foothills of the Rockies, their peaks peeking into the sky above, kids hanging out on beautiful lawns surrounded by huge trees playing music and frisbee—my kind of place.

I find the College of Music. Explaining my unexpected situation to the receptionist, I ask for an audition. Amazingly the voice faculty are meeting now and willing to hear me. Not feeling really prepared or warmed up, part of me wondering what I'm even doing this for —I sing my heart out. The Dean who happens to be there walks me down to his office, shaking my hand and welcoming me.

"Congratulations, Tim! We'll see you in the fall!"

"Don't I have to apply to the university?"

IT MAY BE no surprise that that's where I spent the next three years, finally graduating with a Bachelor of Music Education and a Diploma in Education. But after that audition I had loaded up my black 1970 Datsun 510 station wagon with all my stuff, my big stereo speakers taking up the bulk of the space, and drove from San Francisco to my new university home. Not knowing where I'd stay after the two nights I'd booked at a youth hostel, this was me really leaving home for the first time in my life, heading off alone to find my destiny.

Choosing Boulder from all the places I'd visited all over the country was not an easy choice. There were a lot of places I discovered in my travels that I really liked and felt would be a good fit for me. Going alone was not part of the original plan either. My girlfriend Lisa—a pianist and my accompanist—and I, hoped to find a school that suited both our interests. Boulder was not that place for her, so this choice meant truly leaving behind everything I knew and loved, thrusting myself into the great unknown. It was at once thrilling and terrifying.

More importantly, however, Boulder is where I discovered Jonathan Fox and Jo Salas, founders of Playback Theatre, in my hometown of New Paltz, New York of all places. How did I not know them then? Playback is an original form of improvisational theatre based on the enactment of personal stories shared by the audience. The Boulder troupe solved a problem I'd struggled with since starting college: the physical impossibility of studying both Music Education and Theatre, my original plan. Boulder Playback meant I could simply focus my studies on Music Ed and still scratch that theatre itch.

Perhaps the most important thing about all this is where my life and career went after that. My extensive training and vast experience in Playback led me to starting several companies in order to use theatre as a tool in organizational development and change. My work employs theatre to reflect organizational culture and climate by enacting real workplace situations, the story of the organization. Applying the axiom that the wisdom to solve the challenges in any organization or to change the system inherently exists within the system itself, we'd improvise audience suggestions to potential solutions. This helped them see themselves, then identify agreements, behaviors, commitments, and policies or procedures they could put in place to make the changes they knew they needed.

That led me to the world of leadership development training, including storytelling as a leadership tool and leadership/executive coaching. I've travelled the world, worked with some of the most influential and successful companies, and I've been a guest speaker at the top executive education programs in the US. It led me to the Changing Work Collective and to writing this chapter. Personally it led to meeting my wife, finding my lovely home in the countryside of Western Massachusetts, and an expanded path to consciousness.

All that from one simple moment, one simple choice.

. . .

AS CONSCIOUS BUSINESS leaders it's important to take time to reflect on our personal experiences, especially crucible or defining moments, and to recognize the important lessons we've learned from them that we can apply to various dimensions of our current life and work. Time can reveal many more gifts than we were able to see or learn from when they happened.

Among the many lessons for me in this tale is that the UNC dean encouraged me to trust my own experience, my own inner knowing, including my uncomfortable ambivalence. Somehow some part of me *knew* this was not the right place for me. What part was that? Was I ready to listen to and honor that? At the time, no—I was more concerned about doing it right, pleasing and impressing others, following the "rules", those old inner voices learned from family, society, business.

How do we learn to listen for, recognize, and honor our own inner knowing?

Of all the many voices we hear in our head, thoughts we think, feelings we feel—how do we fully connect with that part of us that can discern what is right for us, our own truth, regardless of what others or the world will tell us? What is the process for being fully connected to what I like to call the *Essential Self*, informed by Roberto Assagioli, M.D., the founder of Psychosynthesis—who referred to "the 'self,' that is to say the point of pure self-awareness, as the *center* of our consciousness?"[1]

In my talks, coaching, and training, I invite people to pay attention to the conditions for connection.

When we have those moments of being fully connected with our Essential Self, where are we?

What is happening around us?

What informs the ability to connect fully in that way?

Playing music of course is one of my conduits to self. Being in nature, especially when hiking, bicycling, cross country skiing, is also a big one for me. Nature and the physical environment are important factors that greatly impact our experiences of learning and development. It seems that the UNC dean knew this. The degree to which we feel comfortable in a place, feel like it's a place we belong and fit in, impacts how we behave and perform. Apple Park in Cupertino, California, for example, was intentionally designed to maximize employees' opportunities for creativity and collaboration.

Have you ever worked in a physical environment that was the opposite of inspiring?

Did it impact the quality of your work or your relationships?

Conversely, think of places where you've been at your best, done your best work, developed trusted relationships. Did the physical structure or environment help create the context for that positive experience?

You might even consider the place where you're reading this book right now. Is it a place that is conducive to learning, growing, and connection? Is there another place that might be better?

THAT DAY in Greeley I took a situation that seemed terrible at first and paused and took a step back to consider my options. An idea came to mind (Boulder), a nudge, and I followed it and took action. Many times I've learned the value of getting an inner nudge then following it to see what I discover.

This is the essence of improvisation. In improvisational theatre a core principle is "Yes, and…" The idea is to accept any "offer" that comes your way and add to it. Individually, if you get an idea, go for it, accept it, and do something to add voice, movement, language, anything to bring it to life. When you're onstage with someone else and they do or say something, instead of blocking, ignoring or disagreeing, you accept it by saying "Yes, and…" then build on it or offer something else, even a different idea. Exercises to practice this improv theatre technique have been used to help organizations and teams with innovation and collaboration. It invites thinking outside the box. This requires curiosity. When something doesn't make sense or seem right, and you don't know what to do, get curious.

I also learned to step up when I most needed to, performing at my best on demand. This involved the physical readiness learned by practice and repetition, using the skills I'd honed over time. It also required being fully present in the moment. There are many practices that help develop this including vipassana meditation, and we learn them in theatre training, especially improvisation.

Personally there are two things that I've learned can help me in any moment. These practices are something you can do too, even now.

Feel your feet in your shoes. There they are! You probably didn't have your attention on your feet a moment ago, but now that you've read this, there they are. Notice what your feet feel like in whatever is covering them, or simply your skin. Feel them on the ground. Put them flat on the floor if they're not already. Notice feeling the floor underneath your feet. Feel that connection to the ground.

Feel your breath in your body. Take a nice big slow full breath in through your nose, and out through your mouth. Where do you notice the breath going in your body? Even just notice the sensation as it passes in through your nose hairs or warming your mouth on the way out. Do it again and notice if anything changes. Does the breath go anywhere different this time? Third time's a charm! Now using this awareness, let yourself breathe naturally, without directing the breath anywhere. Notice where in your body the breath feels most at ease. Where does it naturally want to go by itself, where does it feel like its home? Who is it that's doing the noticing? Could this be your Essential Self? Could this be a place from which you might know what is true for you?

I TRULY FEEL blessed for the way my life has unfolded and the experiences I've had through my work. This leads me to my final point. Gratitude is key. What are you grateful for in your life? Even if you feel a great sense of suffering right now, or feel overwhelmed by the complexities of your current situation and aren't sure what to do, what is one thing you are grateful for? Focus on that.

Remembering these three things may help.

1. **Trust your own inner knowing, even the discomfort, ambivalence, or unhappiness.** It could be a powerful signpost that is trying to tell you something important. Listen to it.
2. **Pause.** Take a step back and try to look at the situation from a broader perspective. Get curious and consider what options may be just down the road that you hadn't yet considered.
3. **When the moment calls for it step up, stay present, and take action.** One of my favorite definitions of courage is to feel the fear and do it anyway. Know and trust that all you've done and learned so far in life has prepared you for this moment. Use the skills you already have and apply them to what is called for now.

These three weave together into one core message: Choose your story.

What do you believe in?

What is important to you?

What do you most want to do, to achieve, to be? How do you know?

If you remain committed to your values and goals, and feel and express gratitude for all you have, even when it doesn't seem like much, life has a way of presenting a way forward.

All you have to do is look for it, listen, and take action.

Tim Van Ness

∽

TIM VAN NESS, PLC is the founder and president of Van Ness & Co. With thirty years leveraging the creative/performing arts for leadership and organizational development, Tim helps organizations live values, develop leaders, and nurture culture. An executive/leadership coach, program designer, expert facilitator and public speaker, his passion is helping people connect with their own voice and inner wisdom. A veteran of Playback Theatre, he's also a singer/songwriter. Tim lives in Western Massachusetts with his wife and cat.

---

1. Assagioli, Roberto. *Psychosynthesis: A collection of basic writings*. Synthesis Center Incorporated, 2000.

TWENTY-THREE

The Adventure of Slowing Down

Courtney Feider

In all of the chaos and haze and noise that is the modern global experience, what if we all felt empowered to slow down?

What if we all felt really engaged in what we were doing, moment to moment?

What if this isn't necessarily a luxury, but a practice and a habit?

For me it began with a lived, potent, and visceral experience. Sadness, trauma, and crisis led me to run away from my college life and I found myself pleasantly lost in twelfth-century cobblestone, wind and rain clouds, the streetside smells of fresh-baking bread, fish markets, bus exhaust, rain and wet cement—all swirled into the unexpected joy of being lost in a moment, but for an extended period of time.

Moving to Edinburgh, Scotland on a whim at age twenty-one, with no previous travel beyond North America, was both a shock and a relief. As a busy student at university, the previous year had seen me balancing a double major and double minor, volunteer work, and a full-time job over breaks. Somewhere in the midst of that, I had also experienced the unexpected loss of a close friend and confidante. All at once the depletion, the unsustainable pace, and the grief caught up to me. I visited the student exchange program office and within a year I was off to Scotland as my place of reprieve.

The extent of my knowledge of the country was limited to a great travel book that I read on the plane ride there. And since it was 1997 there was no research via the internet that would rapidly and artificially fill in the gaps between my expectations and my experience. What I expected was a shifted form of stress, culture-shock, and loneliness. What I found was comfort, safety, satisfaction, and ease.

A great deal of it had to do with how I oriented my questions about the world, the amount of time I spent reflecting and being introspective, and how I took time to process the things that happened to me. Over the six months, during some of the most harrowing weather in a Scottish calendar year, I lived quietly with strangers, I learned gently and without force, I took photographs on film and wouldn't know if I had captured the memories well or not until I returned home months later. And each night when I got home, I wrote it all down.

The state I had been in at home had been frantic, fast, demanding, structured, and exhausting.

A slower pace and reflection were required. In this new state and place, my life took the time it took. I had never felt the freedom of that.

During this time, I intentionally removed myself from the exhaustion I felt when I arrived and I lived in a state of quiet focus. I was experiencing a unique way of living in the moment, accepting what was in front of me with no strain or expectation.

Even as it happened I understood that this was rare and that I would treasure it for the rest of my life. This gift was partially a generational one, partly a circumstantial one—and completely one built on finding a new way of working, on catching the patterns before they caught me, and on softly integrating in real time.

In Scotland at the time, you couldn't find a Starbucks on every corner. You ate traditional and local food. You placed phone calls and waited (sometimes a long time) for a response. You made eye contact and spoke with strangers instead of scrolling.

The Adventure of Slowing Down

Time and space were our allies.
We were deeply present.

I HAVE a real and growing concern that we are losing track of this practice. We in Generation X were given an enormous gift in learning as things unfolded, and this gift can easily become lost as future generations experience extreme speed, access, and global transparency.

The privacy of growth is missing.
And so are the allies of time and space.

IN GEN X, as we were growing up and coming up in work, we were presented with forced resilience because things were constantly and rapidly changing with our world and technology. We lived life in analog and had the luxury of living free from constant distraction and disruption—were afforded the privacy to live life in a personal and quiet way. We formed relationships because we needed to in order to communicate and sometimes with the people who were around the people we wanted to be close to: our friend's parents, or colleagues with whom we need to form a rapport. We used patience to wait for a reply and retained information and learned by writing things down and reading pages and pages of research.

We learned at work how to "climb the ladder" and how to learn from others in front of us, while also forging our own master course in initiative. We worked on our emotional space and intelligence when it wasn't a recognized science, and we formed our own opinions instead of listening to a shrill dialogue.

Safe "space" was our personal way of doing things, peccadillos, secret details that only those close to us knew. We learned to soothe ourselves during heartbreak and learned something new when we needed to make a change. New has been standard for us. We also experienced a great deal of intolerance, massive global shifts, and the consequences of certain amounts of ambiguity and inefficiency.

The modern world is a strange place for my tiny-slice

generation. We are sandwiched between two huge generations and have a lot of quiet wisdom to offer because we are deeply experienced with the flow that accompanies change.

The common ground in all of this? Going slower and being intentional.

Being present.

Time.

Space.

Now we have incredible access to each other worldwide and across many areas and sizes business. We are also inundated by information, and no matter how valuable some of it is, at a certain level of volume it gets difficult to not take it all in as noise. We are an amalgam of the people we spend the most time with and instead of personal relationships, those might be interactions with a team member at work or with a contact on social media.

The distance is tiny, but the chasm is great.

As Baby Boomers and Generation X are beginning to retire, there is a rapidly growing need for younger and very technically adept leaders to step up, but who can they be mentored by? And how can they learn to quiet the noise when the volume is on overdrive?

IT MAY ACTUALLY BE a return to the simple that will save us from the overwhelm. And we may have to help ourselves first instead of relying on workplace mentorship to show us each and every step in real time. Small things become big. Little details become profound change. And needing support becomes conscious collaboration.

We know that an astounding majority of leaders are missing the habit of daily reflection, but those who do take the time to reflect increase their self and social awareness. In their contributions at work they become up to ninety percent more productive and transformational than their peers.

For reflection I still keep a practice from the time I spent in Scotland, and I have modified it for my clients' use as they work to step back from the volume of what they face every day.

I like to recommend keeping a small notebook dedicated to this work and writing it out by hand to activate new neurological connections. This slower writing method can change our relationship with the things we discover.

Here are six questions I believe help us begin to foster a different path. The answers offer us a way of working that is quieter, more intentional, and more focused on a specific outcome.

Do you have a clear goal and a resilient mindset? Focusing on a clear goal streamlines our efforts and reduces distractions. The choice of a resilient and growth-focused mindset allows us to have sustained focus, which is essential for deep, intentional work. It also makes room for us to make mistakes, throw the draft away, and start again.

How much time do you need and what will you spend it on? Emphasizing essential behaviors that keep us focused on time management declutters our schedule, reminiscent of a time when work was less about multitasking and more about meaningful progress. This is a perfect container to create a practice of saying "no" to things that don't (and can't) fit in the day.

Which of your commitments are in competition with one another? Addressing competing commitments clears mental clutter and closes our emotional stress "loops", allowing for a more purposeful approach to regular tasks. This amplifies our focus on effectiveness over efficiency.

What are your underlying assumptions? Choosing to challenge our assumptions (that may feel like facts) helps us to reduce psychological noise and focuses our energy on overcoming real and actual, not perceived, barriers—fostering a work environment that values quality over quantity.

How can you prioritize your energy? Continuously checking on our perceptions versus realities and getting outside perspective keeps our work relevant and focused and prevents overload and open emotional stress cycles. Enormous amounts of time and energy can be saved by working on things piece by piece, and resisting the opportunity to succumbing to the constant connectivity that characterizes the modern workplace.

How will you measure your progress and change? Too much of our measurement these days focuses on perception. Holding a consistent and very simple journaling practice each day can help us to put down what we have worked on, worried about, held by ourselves or with others, and what tomorrow will bring. This helps us to be present with the people we love when we leave work and to flow into the space where we need to rest.

In Scotland this was a mental exercise I did while walking from where I was to where I needed to be. Today I write down the answers to three simple questions at the end of each day, using pen and paper in a dedicated space, and I track the patterns over time.

Ask yourself:

1. What went well?
2. What went badly?
3. What do you need help with?

This gentle querying and journaling practice has helped me separate the abundance of information swirling around me from my experience, and in that gap to find things that help me expand and feel more sovereign in my approach to work and life. These steps are a beginning to helping revive a work style where depth, intention, and focus prevail—reducing distractions and promoting a healthier and more sustainable approach to professional growth and organizational success.

Though I know I can never really relive the relief and peace I felt in Edinburgh in 1997, I also know I don't have to live at the speed of information today. I have the ability to choose how I show up, and so do you.

Your reality is yours to write, and it begins with simplicity and steadiness.

Your allies are time and space.

The Adventure of Slowing Down

Courtney Feider

Courtney Feider, CMT PCC, brings over twenty-five years of corporate experience in leadership and behavioral development, organizational strategy, change management, and business communications. She focuses her work on enterprise and medium to large businesses. Courtney lives in the Pacific Northwest and works with clients from the US, Canada, and the UK.

TWENTY-FOUR

Bridging Worlds

Katherine Twells

It had only been a few months since my medical recovery and my good friend Tracy called to invite me to go with her on an impromptu trip to Greece.

"I need to sort some things out, then I'm leaving tomorrow," she said.

I would have one week to arrive in time to join her on the back half of the trip. Wise and caring counsel by friends told me not to go. What would happen if I had a relapse in a foreign country? That moment forced a decision between fear and joy, and while caution was practical, I had already given much of my life to that stance. The answer was an enthusiastic yes and I found myself standing on a balcony in Santorini overlooking the Aegean Sea, filled with expansive possibility for what life could offer.

Rewind to six months earlier. I can't sleep because my body is not at peace. It's three in the morning and dark in the hospital room except for the small blinking lights on the monitors. There is an occasional beep from those same machines, those that are making sure life is stable inside the room, even though it was far from stable inside my mind. There is a deep silence, and my inner voice starts in: *How did I get here? Will I ever return to a normal life?* It is well before the invention of the iPhone, so I put a cassette of mixed music into a Sony Walkman and put the earphones in. I get lost in the lyrics, and for a moment I am timeless and free from the pain and uncertainty.

That hospital room was not where a twenty-nine-year-old wanted to be on a Saturday night, but there was something there for me to discover. On that night and in the days after, I came to realize that our choice in every moment is to decide whether we are the hero or the victim of the story that only we can write. My emergency surgery was a catalytic plot twist, but as is true with many of us, the seeds of my lessons were planted far earlier and their essence realized far later.

As a middle child I was born into the role of harmonizer, finding my voice between an older sibling who was strong, steady, and a natural leader, and a younger one (my Irish twin) who was the first boy of the family and seemed to roll with things with greater ease. My pathway was somewhat unremarkable as I dutifully followed the playbook—good grades, work hard, stay out of trouble. Then college, job, and marriage. I learned what was expected and how to gain acceptance.

There is nothing wrong with the blueprint so many of us follow, as it offers great gifts and experiences. But it's the nuance, the unconscious inner knowing that we bring forward, that starts to reveal what we must learn. Questions about meaning and purpose often go unanswered. If we are too busy following a prescribed recipe for success, we often drown out that subtle voice of wisdom. Our navigation systems are given at birth, yet life has a way of leading us down distracting roads that can be far from what is intended. The chaos of the external world so easily drowns out the inner guidance that calls us to new revelations. There are voices of people we admire, love, and respect. Surely they know what is best for us. But as we play the role we believe we need to play, there is a whisper of discontent which if unacknowledged moves into a scream, as we find ourselves lost in confusion or asking questions from a dark hospital room at three in the morning.

Yet sometimes getting lost is also being found. The unexpected jolts that catalyze the deeper questions seem strangely orchestrated to help us crack the code. After all, great movies show the hero in trouble, and we are at the edge of our seats to see the resolution! All we really need to do is answer the call and have the courage to stay curious and compassionate. The events in our lives are signposts and the adventure is in the unfolding.

MY ILLNESS at twenty-nine plunged me into a fascinating journey of discovering the connection with mind and body. I was determined to learn well and live differently. After my recovery and grand adventure in Greece, I entertained thoughts of leaving my job in the corporate world to teach yoga or meditation. New knowledge was casting me deeper and deeper into the mysteries of the body and the way we shape our lives through the power of our thoughts. This was long before it was mainstream, so it felt like an exciting new frontier. But that was not what destiny had in store. Incredible mentors at my company not only welcomed me back with confidence but challenged me to tackle a leadership role. I found a great sense of meaning in seeing others grow and as time went on I knew that coming close to death was an invitation to become more alive. I started to bridge very different worlds. One as a corporate leader working to meet tangible business results and another on a deep spiritual journey into the awareness of what must be healed to uncover the parts of us that are begging to be seen and celebrated. I found that I loved being immersed in both and that they each informed the other.

Judi Neal, PhD, coined the word 'edgewalkers'.[1] These are people who walk between worlds and have the ability to build bridges between them. They have a strong inner life yet are effective in the everyday demands of the external. Edgewalkers choose to look at unlikely intersection points and to the future for unseen emerging possibilities. Bridging worlds means seeing how everything connects and how meaning is found in the small moments where we meet the ordinary with a sense of deeper awareness. Buddhism refers to non-monastics as "householders"—

people who live a normal life yet are still seekers of enlightenment.

I don't believe you need to obtain enlightenment to live a life of greater peace.

What if the essence of changing everything was for each of us to evolve exactly where we are in our own unique timing?

What if we remembered and courageously spoke in our true voice? Not the voice of culture or influencers or any other standard, but the one that is informed from the heart.

What if we refused the labels that are designed to fit us into categorized boxes? As we step into the essence of who we truly are we inspire others to do the same and that is where our greatest collective potential unfolds.

In this state of wholeness, we quiet the voice inside us that demands performance—the one that says our accomplishments are an internal prerequisite for love and acceptance. We come to know that we are loved for our being and not for our doing. Perhaps the path of redemption in this life is to finally honor our place in the great mystery and to accept that to be here is enough—choosing in each moment to become the best of ourselves. As much as we long to arrive, we are ever evolving and growing, and the unfinished raw edges make everything more interesting and more beautiful.

NOW, after a corporate career that has spanned more than thirty-five years, and knowing that our inner journey informs everything that happens in the outward evolving drama, I have found the richness of bridging different worlds.

The journey is not a dualistic choice of only one environment. Everything is intertwined. My company has given me the trust and freedom to create events and programming that have included invitations into the inner landscape, into compassion and humanity. Through the birth of my sons and the inevitable twists and turns of life, I have found the most supportive love and connection in the often chaotic world of work.

Our practice is how we show up in every moment with those

around us. No matter how we choose to spend our lives we are human first and there are so many moments available to us to express who we really are. I have met beautiful souls in the corporate world as I witnessed them finding their own true voice. In business we are learning to take down our masks and embrace our fundamental humanity and in doing that we unleash creativity and connection.

There is more joy and ease when we are not exhausted by the pursuit of perfection. We begin to see that risk-taking and failure teach us how to succeed. In my corporate career I continue to walk the edge of driving growth and profit and inviting others into the inner landscape of building resilience and conscious action. That resilience and action come full circle back into growth and into profit grounded in integrity. A conscious flywheel is born rippling out into creation.

Since we are wonderfully human, sometimes we forget and there is static in the frequency. In the moment we may feel like we are failing, yet the old patterns are calling us back again to wake up to what matters. Building bridges and merging worlds can be disorienting because there are so many voices in the mix: old stories to release and new ones to be written. Healing our wounds requires more than understanding what is on the surface; it's a deeper exploration into what caused us to get there in the first place. If we do not answer these questions, we are bound to find ourselves repeating the curriculum.

For me this has been a journey into my own truth and voice. Both my leadership and parenting are informed by a love for the mystery of this grand experience and by the invitation to others to engage in the most fruitful work of their lives—to know that their purpose is to live authentic to their true selves. When we are told from a young age that to survive is to fit in it takes courage and a willingness to be different. It is a process of trusting that your song has its own frequency; when combined with others willing to sing authentically, a symphony emerges.

Movies and myths drop hints on the power that lies within us. The yellow brick road led to a man behind the curtain and each character had what they needed all along. For some reason we believe the answers are outside of us or somewhere in the distant future. And while there are mentors, coaches, and leaders that can reveal blind spots and unlock potential, there is an important place for our own inner navigation.

My question to you is this: do you see your own wholeness? Do you know who you are, what you care about and how you serve? I believe we have the answer even if the wisdom gets buried under programming that is not our own. The journey of a lifetime is to chip away at what does not belong to us in order to uncover our true essence—our ability to occupy the space that is perfectly designed for us. Freedom is a way of being. We imprison ourselves in chains of perception and belief, yet truth is there—underneath it all—waiting to be embraced and lived. Do not wait for someone else to set you free.

I AM STANDING CLOSE to the edge. The impromptu trip to Greece ushers in an impractical adventure. I am on the balcony watching the sun glisten on an expansive sea and I feel so far from that hospital room. I am on the edge, talking about vulnerability, overwhelm, and resilience—when the business asks about profit and loss. I know they are entwined, and that human flourishing is the key to growth—that conscious business can change the world one courageous human at a time.

The irony is that sometimes walking to the edge might lead us right back to the middle. I have spent much of my time bridging worlds that in truth cannot be disconnected. Like the incredible workings of the human body and the vastly interconnected systems in nature, everything we do affects the total creation. The health of the one is the health of the whole. Like rising above a situation to see it in a new light, we come to know that the work we do to become our full selves affects the web of life. We all touch. Our power is in the integration and knowing that it all works for our good.

If I were to leave you with some small steps that inform this journey I would guide you in three ways:

First, be willing to be still and listen to the voices inside. We are often drowned in distraction from the outer world. The more you do this, the more space you will find between stimulus and response. You become the wise observer.

Second, live courageously in your true essence. Invest upfront in the contemplation of the values of your heart and in the stand you choose to make in the world. It may require being a dissenting voice, but you will know you played the part you needed to play.

And third, have compassion for yourself and others on the journey. It is an unfolding evolution of deeper and deeper truths that illuminate the way. When you feel lost, trust in the synchronicities that inform new directions and know that you will be shown something that will serve and guide. And do not forget to see the joy even in confusion. It is always there when we have eyes to see.

We are not meant to walk alone. There is a beautiful mystery in the winding road; sometimes I lift you and sometimes you lift me. We can walk to the edge together and discover more of why we choose the adventure in the first place. Perhaps then we will discover that the truth we have been seeking was inside us the entire time.

Katherine Twells

∼

KATHERINE TWELLS has enjoyed thirty-five years in the corporate arena at The Coca-Cola Company. Currently serving as Vice President, West Region she advocates intrapreneurship—the art of creation inside organizational structure. She is the architect of The Compassion Lab, which serves to promote emotional agility and wisdom in the workplace and which hosts The Compassion Lab Podcast, exploring the power of conscious leadership and the interconnectivity of all things.

---

1. Neal, Judi. *Edgewalkers: People and organizations that take risks, build bridges, and break new ground.* Bloomsbury Publishing USA, 2006.

TWENTY-FIVE

Operating From Your Zone of Genius

Earl Talbot

"There's more to life than this, there's more to life than this." The mantra was drumming again and again, beating in the center of my chest and drowning out all noise from the open-plan office of nearly a hundred people.

"What's happening to me?" I thought. "Is this what it feels like to have a panic attack?"

I was at my desk with that mantra relentlessly pounding away, looking around to see if anyone noticed the chaos that was happening inside. Without thinking, I stood up and started walking, not knowing where I was going. I ended up in the office of Chris Colgan, the director of customer services. I didn't know him well, we had only had a few interactions, but for some strange reason I felt he was the only one I could speak to at this point.

"I don't know what I'm doing here," I said, sitting down. "But I needed to speak to someone."

As I began to describe what was happening to me he listened intently and asked me a few questions before handing me a flyer for a retreat called Soul Recharge in Sedona, Arizona.

"Can I borrow that flyer for a while?" I asked him.

"Okay," he said.

I took the flyer. Went away. Thirty minutes later I came back to Chris' office.

"I'm there!" I announced.

"Wait! What do you mean, you're there?"

"I booked my flight."

"Have you spoken to the lady who's running the retreat to see if there's a spot for you?"

"Don't worry about that," I said. "That's just the details. I'm going to be there."

And that was the decision that changed the course of my life.

It was the year 2000 and it was The Wild West for the internet in the United Kingdom. Everybody wanted it, even if they didn't know what it was. I had started my role as a tele-sales representative twelve months earlier at a U.K.-based internet company.

I was doing really well, smashing my targets as the top salesperson. You didn't even need to be good at sales to be able to sell the internet at the time, but I already had sales experience and that gave me an edge. Life was going well. I was living in my new apartment with my new girlfriend and earning good money.

This was in stark contrast to the life I had been living nearly two years before, when I was depressed and technically homeless. Luckily a kind family member took me in, but this was a dark time for me. I felt I was in a hole that I could not get out of. I didn't want to eat or get out of bed. It was only through some honest and tough conversations with myself, and through feeling guilty for being a burden to my cousin, that I came out of the slump and focused on getting the job that I now had.

So what was happening to me that day I reached out to Chris just didn't make sense. I should have been happy, but I had this deep sense of unfulfillment in the pit of my stomach and that mantra repeating itself, booming in the center of my chest:

"There is more to life than this!"

Soul Recharge

Operating From Your Zone of Genius

THE RETREAT TOOK place six weeks after my conversation with Chris and we had arranged to travel together.

We arrived in Phoenix then drove a couple of hours to get to Sedona. I had never heard of this place before seeing his flyer. After a few days there I realized it was a beautiful and famous place, with its red rocks and crystals literally growing out of the ground, where many Westerns were filmed. But it was the vortex's energy centers that made it an energy-healing Mecca for 'spiritual' people from all over the world, including us.

I had no expectations for the retreat, as I had never even heard of one before. To be honest I was skeptical. I felt like it was going to be a tree-hugging hippy fest, but I trusted that I was there for a reason and importantly I would have tried anything at that point.

There were about ten of us on the retreat, a mix of men and women all from the U.K.. The retreat leader, Caroline Reynolds, was a Welsh lady who had given up her corporate career and now was guiding people to "spiritual fitness", which was also the name of her book.[1]

The retreat itself was a mix of experiences, including a Native American sweat lodge ceremony, angel drawing and reading, kinesiology, hot stone massages, and some group workshops. All of these were new experiences and I didn't know what these activities were meant to do for me and still had a high dose of skepticism. But even apart from the transcendent experience of the hot stone massage, my first massage ever, I was hooked.

As we were nearing the end of the retreat I started to notice something was changing. I can't say exactly what and when it changed, but something shifted in me. I started to notice I felt lighter. It was like loosening a straitjacket that I wore on the inside; I could start to breathe properly again, letting in air and life.

I started to notice the distinctions between my thoughts and feelings and different emotions I was experiencing. Before I had arrived I felt as though I carried around inside me one massive knotted ball of stuff (thoughts, emotions, stress) over which I had no control. Now that ball was slowly unraveling, creating space in which I could see the distinction of the different elements.

These elements, the new things of which I was becoming aware, weren't just happening to me outside of my control. I recognized them as aspects of myself, elements operating for my benefit. A few years later I termed this process "Inner-standing", borrowing the idea from Rastafarians whom I knew. While the meaning may be different from Rasta's own, I think it encapsulates the same essence.

The Return

I CAN'T SAY that the Soul Recharge retreat cured me, but it certainly awakened something in me that had, and continues to have, a profound impact. I've been back to Sedona a few times and even co-facilitated my first Vision Quest retreat there with Chris. I never had another episode like that day in the office of my existential crisis. In fact I now see that experience as my awakening.

What I realized was that in my determination not to go back to that state of depression I had disconnected from my inner wisdom. That mantra drumming inside of me was the parts of me that I had disconnected from by not being consciously aware of them. These elements were basically screaming at me to wake up and be aware.

Over the next two decades I built upon my awareness, language, and practices to develop strategies for what I now call mindset code-breaking.

The elements that I became aware of in the retreat I now refer to as the 5 Intelligences:

- Cognitive Intelligence (IQ): the logical, rational, intellectual aspect of the mind.
- Emotional Intelligence (EQ): governs the emotional aspects of the mind.
- Somatic/Physical Intelligence (PQ): governs the physicality aspect of the mind.
- Intuitive Intelligence (iQ): governs the innate and instinctual aspect of the mind.

- Holistic/Spiritual (SQ): governs the energetic interconnectedness of the mind.

SINCE THE INDUSTRIAL Revolution we have been biased toward IQ. This bias has increased with the rise of knowledge workers. This bias is an issue because often it is at the expense of the other four intelligences.

It's important to state that the mind referred to here is not the brain. Rather the brain is an element or organ of the mind, and in this way the mind can be viewed as a whole system of various intelligences.

Imagine the mind as a guitar. Each string, fret, and chord represents a different intelligence of the mind. Our conscious awareness is like the guitarist who plucks and strums the strings to create myriad melodies and harmonies. Routine upgrades to the mind are akin to tuning and maintaining the guitar, ensuring it remains finely tuned and capable of producing its full spectrum of emotional, intuitive, somatic, spiritual, and cognitive expressions.

We all have access to the wisdom of the "Five Intelligences" but we ignore them at our peril. When we're struggling with thoughts and emotions or reacting in ways that don't seem right, there is something deeper going on. Usually the source of discomfort, doubt, confusion, etc. is a signal or an invitation to look inside for deeper inner-standing. In this moment, by bringing our awareness back into the various intelligences of the mind, we're effectively re-tuning ourselves back into alignment.

Let me give you an example. Have you ever suffered from imposter syndrome? Or had a scenario in which you are doubting yourself when there is no reason to?

You are likely to focus on how you are feeling about these situations, especially if the reaction is a strong one like feeling sick or being hot and flustered or having shallow breathing. At this point you are consciously aware of your somatic intelligence. But what you may not be consciously aware of is the negative thoughts and inner dialogue that are coming from the cognitive intelligence that generates the emotions that translate into visceral feelings. Or, when you have a gut feeling about something, using your intuitive intelligence (iQ), you might override it using your cognitive intelligence (IQ). Later when you get additional information, you'll say to yourself, "I knew it, why didn't I listen to myself?" The thing is, you did listen to yourself, just not to the aspect of the mind that had the wisdom.

The main issue arises from misalignment of the intelligences, and this happens when either we ignore them or act in ways that conflict with our inner wisdom. The invitation that comes from being aware of the symptoms described above is to bring our whole self-back to a place of alignment. And when we're wholly or mostly in alignment, we're operating in our zone of genius.

This is like the guitarist who has mastered their craft and can seemingly pick up a guitar and play effortlessly in their genius zone. Anyone who plays will understand how much practice this takes. The same things apply here—from working out and intentional movement, yoga, breathwork, eating healthily, walking in nature, reading inspirational books, to practicing mindfulness. While we may not need to do all of these all the time, we usually need to optimize two or three of the Five Intelligences on a consistent basis.

Most of us will have glimpses and moments of operating in a genius zone, but it's not so often that we find people who do this consistently and at a high level. This requires significant discipline towards rituals and practices and for this reason it's quite rare to find people who do, like Leonardo da Vinci, Michael Jordan, Jimi Hendrix, Adele, Albert Einstein.

So what can we do to bring things back into balance and alignment?

Inner-standing is the starting point of real empowerment, of moving toward self-leadership. It comes from awareness of these intelligences and the roles they play in our system, just like understanding how to play the guitar. For me this all starts with slowing down and breathing, then pausing, then deeply listening to self—the sum of the "Five Intelligences"—and noticing what I'm becoming aware of in that moment.

This is the genius of the innate wisdom that is designed by the same intelligence that created the universe. We don't have to think about beating our heart or balancing the pH level of our bodies. But we do need to pay attention and see where we are being counterproductive in our lives due to the stresses of modern living —life admin, poor dietary choices, general sedentary lifestyles. We don't need to try to improve upon or change our nature, just tune into what is required now, whether that is rest, hydration, talking to a loved one, or watching a sunset.

The real art is remembering and harnessing the power of your awareness and the only questions you need to answer are: What do you pay attention to? And do you remember to slow down, pause, listen, and inner-stand yourself?

Earl Talbot

∽

EARL TALBOT, founder of Creative Muscle, empowers corporate citizens and solopreneurs to live on purpose. With over twenty-five years in sales and management consulting in the tech sector, he excels at transforming companies and individuals. A certified trainer of neurolinguistic programming, Earl blends ancient wisdom with modern techniques to recode mindsets. Since 2002 he has facilitated wellbeing retreats and mentored teams, unlocked genius, inspired action, and built resilience.

---

1. Reynolds, Caroline. *Spiritual Fitness.* Baca, 2005.

Afterword

As we bring *Leading with Self-Awareness: Starting from the Inside Out* to a close, we find ourselves reflecting deeply on the stories shared within these pages. We can learn so much about our own lives by hearing the stories of others. The themes uncovered by these twenty-five remarkable individuals are not only a collection of vulnerable personal experiences; they are a testament to the power of self-awareness and the transformative potential it holds for each of us.

When we embarked on this endeavor (starting Changing Work), we knew we wanted to create a space where self-awareness could be explored, understood, and embraced as a fundamental pillar of conscious leadership and meaningful work. We dream of workplaces where people feel truly seen, valued, and empowered to bring their whole selves to the table. The narratives shared here underscore the belief that such workplaces are not only possible but imperative for a thriving, compassionate, and equitable world.

Through the lenses of vulnerability, courage, and introspection, our contributors have illuminated the path to self-awareness with authenticity and grace. They have shown us that self-awareness is not a destination but a continuous journey—a journey that requires us to look inward, to confront our fears, to embrace our strengths and weaknesses, and to cultivate a deeper understanding of who we are and how we show up in the world.

As we read each of these authors' stories, we are reminded of the profound truth that change begins within. It is our own self-awareness that serves as the catalyst for broader transformation. When we understand ourselves better, we can lead with empathy, foster genuine connections, and create environments where everyone can flourish. This inner work is the foundation upon which we build not only successful careers but also meaningful lives. We can lead by example and invite others to join us.

In the ever faster-paced, often ambiguous world of work, it is easy to lose sight of the bigger picture. We can become so focused on external achievements and benchmarks that we forget to nurture our inner selves. Yet, as the stories in this book reveal, it is in moments of quiet introspection, of mystical self-surrender, of lifequakes, and of honest self-assessment that we find our true power and purpose.

Our hope is that this book has inspired you to continue your own journey of self-awareness. The path may be challenging, but it is also rich with opportunities for growth, connection, and impact. Whether you are a seasoned leader, an emerging professional, or a conscious-curious human simply seeking greater fulfillment in your work and life, know that you are not alone.

We invite you to carry forward the lessons learned here. Let them guide you in creating workplaces that are not just profitable but also purposeful, where success is measured not only by financial gains but by the positive impact we have on each other and our communities. Let them remind you that every small act of self-awareness and conscious leadership contributes to a larger movement—one that has the power to change work and, ultimately, to change the world.

Thank you for joining us on this journey. May you continue to lead with self-awareness, to embrace your unique path, and to inspire others to do the same.

You can learn more, deepen your skills, find a community of

Afterword

others on the path, and help grow the changing work movement by visiting us at www.changingwork.org.

Let's change work from the inside out together.

With gratitude and hope,

Nicholas Whitaker
Scott Shute
Co-founders - Changing Work

Afterword

Scott Shute

∼

SCOTT SHUTE is the founder of Changing Work. His mission is to change work from the inside out. He blends his experience as a Silicon Valley executive (LinkedIn) with his lifelong practice and passion as a wisdom seeker and teacher. Scott is the author of the award-winning book *The Full Body Yes*.

Afterword

Nicholas Whitaker

~

NICHOLAS WHITAKER is the co-founder of Changing Work and a conscious leadership activist. With over 20 years in tech, media, and entrepreneurship, he deeply understands today's work environment complexities. He is dedicated to promoting conscious business and leadership. Nicholas also works as a well-being and performance coach and is a certified mindfulness meditation facilitator. He lives in the foothills of the Rocky Mountains in Colorado with his wife and three cats.

About Changing Work

Changing Work is a movement deeply committed to revolutionizing the dynamics of the workplace from within.

Our Vision is to **Change Work from the Inside Out.**

Essentially, we are here to make work a more humane, conscious, and nurturing environment; an experience that promotes personal growth, self-awareness, and compassion, while continuing to deliver value to all stakeholders. We recognize that profitability is important, and that it comes with a need for balance not only for shareholders but also for employees, customers, and the broader global community—a world that works for everyone.

Changing Work is a collective of business leaders, employees, coaches, and consultants. Fundamentally, we do two things:

First, we build community. There's something incredibly powerful about being on a journey together with people who are bonded by a desire for a common good. One of our favorite things is our monthly community meeting. There's so much love in the room!

Second, we share best practices. This comes in many forms, including the book in your hands right now. We also have a podcast, a newsletter, courses, cohort-based learning, and so much more.

Have something you'd like to share? Or something you'd like to learn? Or would you just like to be surrounded by like-hearted people?

Come join us at **www.changingwork.org**

Printed in Great Britain
by Amazon